HEARTS OF OAK

The Human Tragedy of HMS Royal Oak

DILIP SARKAR

AMBERLEY

For the late John Anthony, our friend and neighbour, a sailor in both world wars who inspired my childhood with tales of derring-do and adventure on the high seas. Never forgotten, I just wish that this amazing man could have seen this book.

Also for my son, James Sarkar and step-son, George Ainsworth, two young adults full of promise – like many of those tragically lost on HMS Royal Oak.

First published 2010

Amberley Publishing Plc
Cirencester Road, Chalford,
Stroud, Gloucestershire, GL6 8PE

www.amberleybooks.com

Copyright text & pictures © Dilip Sarkar, 2010

The right of Dilip Sarkar to be identified as the Author of this work has been asserted in accordance with the Copyrights, Designs and Patents Act 1988.

ISBN 978 1 84868 944 2

British Library Cataloguing in Publication Data.

A catalogue record for this book is available from the British Library.

Typeset in 12pt on 15pt Sabon.
Typesetting by Fonthill.
Printed in the UK.

Contents

Introduction

All my life I have been fascinated by the Second World War, particularly regarding the experiences of survivors and the deeply moving stories of casualties. The war was a massive interruption, of course, to normality, and ordinary people found themselves plunged into the most extraordinary circumstances, responding accordingly and both experiencing and achieving the hitherto impossible. Take, for example, the story of Air Vice-Marshal Johnnie Johnson, the RAF's top-scoring fighter pilot 1939-45: before the war, Johnnie worked in a borough surveyor's office; by VE Day, he was a highly decorated group captain with 38½ enemy aircraft to his credit, a veritable legend in his own lifetime. The casualties, of course, reflected quite the opposite, their vitality and potential snuffed out in an instance, depriving them of life's great opportunities and mankind of their contribution. Sacrifices such as these were made to preserve democracy and keep the world free from Nazi oppression. They should never be forgotten, and yet, although we have war memorials scattered throughout the land recording names of the dead, the actual likenesses of casualties are in the process of being lost and forgotten. As time moves on, they sadly pass from even their families' living memory. It is with that fact very much in mind, therefore, that I came to write this book.

In 1999, at the comparatively late age of thirty-eight, I became a recreational scuba diver.

1. The island of Hoy, shrouded in mist and photographed as MV *Halton* heads into the Flow for another day diving the German High Seas Fleet in 2005.

2. The reminders of war are omnipresent around Scapa Flow: pillboxes and lookout posts, now empty and silent sentinels.

3. The highly experienced technical diver and instructor Elwyn Harper, of Seastyle, Worcester, rejoins the boat after another enjoyable dive at Scapa Flow. (Lesley Harper).

4. Lesley Harper photographing the German cruiser *Köln*. (Elwyn Harper).

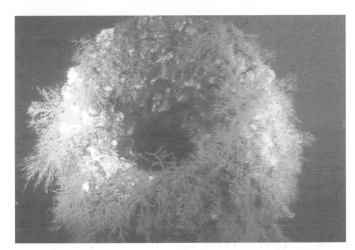

5. One of the German ship's guns, covered in soft corals. (Elwyn Harper).

6. The author in training at Stoney Cove for the 2003 'Seastyle' expedition to Scapa Flow. (Gordon Lawley).

7. The famous battle-cruiser HMS *Hood* at the Scapa Flow anchorage.

8. HMS *Royal Oak*.

The reason for this was to pursue my interest in maritime history and archaeology, and, over the years since, I have dived many wrecks from both twentieth-century global conflicts. In June 2003, I went on a trip with my diving club, 'Seastyle' of Worcester, to dive the German High Seas Fleet wrecks at Scapa Flow.

9. The buoy marking the wreck of HMS *Royal Oak*. This picture clearly shows the close proximity of land.

Every previous dive had been for that moment, and I was not disappointed. The Orkneys are steeped in naval history, and I immediately felt an affinity with the place. The diving was superb, and actually being able to see and touch great old dreadnoughts like the *Markgraff* and *Krownprinz Wilhelm* was an almost indescribable thrill.

That week, we lived aboard the MV *Halton,* out of Stromness and expertly skippered by Bob Anderson, who shared an interest in the history of Scapa with Elwyn Harper, the founder and proprietor of Seastyle, and me. Knowing of my great interest in U-boat operations, and, of course, the story of U-47 penetrating Scapa's supposedly impregnable defences in 1939 and sinking HMS *Royal Oak,* one day, between dives, Bob took us out to the green buoy marking the old battleship's last resting place. I knew that 833 men had been lost that fateful night in October 1939, when *Royal Oak* sank in just a few minutes.

10. The marker buoy, marked with wreaths and flowers.

To be afloat there, where this tragedy occurred, to see the wreaths and notes of remembrance from relatives wired to the buoy, and to see just how close to land this awful thing had happened was extremely moving and left an indelible impression.

Whilst at Scapa, Elwyn and I visited just about every museum on the Orkneys, learning more about HMS *Royal Oak,* and I bought a number of books dealing with the sinking. Almost exclusively, however, those books concentrated on telling the overall story, some in great detail (H. J. Weaver's *Nightmare at Scapa Flow* being superb). None made much reference to the actual casualties, however, so it seemed to me that this omission should be put right. Upon return home, I immediately began researching HMS *Royal Oak,* and thanks to Peter Rowlands (webmaster of www.hmsroyaloak.co.uk) and Ken Toop, a survivor of

11. The bell of HMS *Royal Oak*, preserved in St Magnus Cathedral, Kirkwall, as a memorial to the men who died.

the tragedy and secretary of the HMS *Royal Oak* Association, I was soon in contact with many families who had lost ancestors on the ship. From them I was able to glean photographs and information, the end result of which process is presented here. The intention is for those casualties featured in this book to be representative of the entire crew, as clearly, after such a passage of time, it would be impossible to trace the relatives of all 833. So, at least now we have some record of their likeness, and know what kind of men they were. Although that is clearly the main purpose of this book, I have also re-told the story of HMS *Royal Oak*'s demise, as, from time to time, it does no harm for an oft told story to be reconsidered and freshly presented, keeping it alive in public consciousness.

One thing that also impressed me whilst researching these accounts was the trials and tribulations of the widows left behind, many of whom struggled hard to feed hungry mouths and keep their families together. This led to contact with the War Widows' Association, the AGM of which I had the honour to address in 2005. No expression of respect could be too great regarding these very special ladies, so this book is also a small tribute to them too.

Unfortunately, all these years later, British servicemen are still in harm's way, this time fighting different enemies both at home and on the far side of the world. To conclude, I would use the words of my old friend Martin Drewes in Brazil, a former German night-fighter 'ace' with the coveted Knight's Cross to his credit: 'Now, as then, the world is suffering; will mankind never learn?'

Dilip Sarkar MBE FRHistS. Worcester. March 2009

I

A Dangerous Peace

Surprisingly, given subsequent events, Germany was late to show interest in the first 'diving boats' which appeared early in the twentieth century. For example, by 1908, Germany had but two experimental submarines, whilst the underwater fleets of both Britain and France numbered over sixty apiece. The Imperial German Navy, however, guided by the visionary von Tirpitz, built a modern fleet of battleships and cruisers, mighty dreadnoughts intended to challenge the Royal Navy's long accepted supremacy of the waves. In the event, during the First World War, neither the Royal Navy nor Britain's crucial nautical supply lines were significantly threatened by the Kaiser's surface fleet: the real threat, ironically, came from beneath the sea. German submarines – *unterseeboots* and hence 'U-boats' – wreaked havoc upon Britain's merchant shipping, sending 18 million tons of it to the seabed. Such a figure reflects, in fact, the near severance of this island's supply lines and the very real threat of starvation.

U-boats were able to stalk their quarry, hidden beneath the waves, sinking their victims with torpedoes before disappearing back into the void. As the Great War went on, though, the Royal Navy responded to this menace by introducing the depth-charge and convoy system (the latter, which concentrated merchant ships together). As U-boats operated individually, this tactic significantly reduced the chance of interception, and the depth charge meant that should a U-boat be

12. During the First World War, the U-boat was established as a much-feared weapon, stalking the sealanes and ambushing merchantmen bringing essential supplies to island England. From the album of U-boat veteran Friedrich Pohl, this snapshot shows crewmen of U-25 at sea.

detected, a weapon now existed with which to destroy it. By the autumn of 1917, the U-boat threat had been neutralised and Britain's sea lanes were safe once more.

Previous to the emergence of Germany as a serious sea power before the Great War, Britain's great naval bases, like Portsmouth and Devonport, were on the South Coast, facing France, the natural enemy of that day. The threat posed by the Kaiser's fleet, however, indicated that, in the event of hostilities, the North Sea too would become a battleground. Suitable bases were therefore required in the north: in 1903, Rosyth and Cromarty were opened as such, but the main northern anchorage did not open until 1912, at Scapa Flow, one of the largest natural harbours in the world and situated in the Orkney Islands.

13. A British merchant ship going down, a victim of U-25.

The name Scapa (pronounced 'scappa'), is derived from the ancient Norse word *skalpr* (scabbard) or *skalpei* (ship or isthmus), and Flow from *floi* or *fljot* (large expanse of water). Many a dragon-headed Viking longship had put into this safe anchorage for repairs and rest. In 1263, the Norsemen were defeated and the 'Western Isles' were incorporated into the Kingdom of Scotland. During the early twentieth century, the Admiralty recognised that Scapa Flow enjoyed three distinct and vital advantages as the site for a major naval base: there was room for the entire Grand Fleet, the insular position protected against the attention of spies, and, it was believed, the hydro graphic circumstances of the approaches made submarine attack virtually impossible. Indeed, at that time, with the submarine's potential largely unrecognised, the only perceived danger was from German surface craft operating out of Norway. Security would be provided by sinking obsolete ships to block narrow gaps, and guarding those remaining. Scapa would, therefore, be somewhere ships' crews could relax, safe in the knowledge that their anchorage was impregnable.

Nonetheless, early on in the Great War, as Rear-Admiral H. W. Grant later wrote, 'At that time, Scapa Flow was not a healthy place to live in, because we were never quite sure whether the Hun would get a submarine in. We had a good many scares and had to raise steam. At that time we had not such appliances as depth charges.'

On 23 November 1914, *Kapitänleutnant (Kaleun)* Heinrich von Henning navigated U-18 around the east coast of Orkney and far enough westward to see only a few small ships in Hoxa Sound (Admiral Jellicoe having sent his capital ships to Loch Ewe). His periscope sighted, von Henning was pursued by destroyers and trawlers, but evaded detection by simply lying quietly on the seabed. Upon surfacing, U-18 had the misfortune to be in collision with the trawler *Dorothy Grey* (although some say the submarine was deliberately rammed). The damaged U-boat crash-dived and headed east before hitting a rock, surfacing and being rammed by another trawler, this time the *Kaphedra*. Diving and running again, U-18 had nearly made the safe open water of the Moray Firth when the ill-fated submarine hit the Skerries. Von Henning now had no choice but to surface his crippled vessel and surrender to the Royal Navy.

In December 1914, a boom was fitted across Hoxa Sound, and within a few months similar defences were completed in Switha and Hoy Sounds. Blockships were sunk, minefields laid, and lookout posts strategically positioned around the Flow. Significantly, hydrophones able to detect engine noise and connected to the new depth charge were also installed. Later, cables were laid across the seabed which detected vessels passing overhead. This system was attached to minefields, which, in the event of an unfriendly detection, would be detonated.

In 1916, Admiral Jellicoe had defeated the German surface fleet at Jutland, so by 1917 and the U-boats' defeat, the German Navy was fatally afflicted with poor morale. Halfway through 1918, it was obvious to all that Germany had lost the war. The Kaiser's navy reckoned on one last, desperate throw of the dice: sending a U-boat into Scapa Flow, briefed to sink as many British capital ships as possible before the German High Seas Fleet ventured forth for one last dramatic and decisive battle with the Royal Navy. It was felt that even if Germany lost this proposed engagement, a certain amount of face and pride would at least be restored. The submarine chosen for this suicide mission was UB-116, commanded by *Leutnant* H. J. Emsmann, who was briefed to execute his objective regardless of any risks to his crew (of thirty-three ratings and four officers) and vessel. German intelligence suggested that as the Royal Navy regularly entered and left the Flow via Hoxa Sound, this was unlikely to be defended by mines or other obstructions and so it was here that Emsmann should penetrate the anchorage. The Germans were unaware that the Grand Fleet had already been dispersed around other bases, and so even if Emsmann did achieve the Flow undetected, there was actually little damage that his eleven torpedoes could inflict. Unaware of this, the determined Emsmann pressed on.

At 8.21 p.m. on the evening of 28 October 1918, the Stanger Head hydrophones detected engine noises. As no friendly vessels were known to be in the area, the minefields were activated and the defenders patiently awaited events. At 10.30 p.m., Emsmann peered

14. The once-proud German High Seas Fleet interned at Scapa Flow.

through his periscope and, no doubt, noted with pride and satisfaction that UB-116 was perfectly positioned within the Flow and adjacent to the Hoxa boom. The German's jubilation was short lived, however: his tiny periscope had been sighted by a searchlight crew and reported. Minutes later, the mines were detonated and UB-116 went to a watery grave at Pan Hope. Emsmann's mission was clearly both futile and impossible. The demise of UB-116 an absolute and complete waste of human life which achieved nothing. Just thirteen days later, Germany surrendered, making UB-116 the last U-boat to be destroyed in the First World War (and also the first to be destroyed by way of a remotely controlled minefield).

Although the war was over, Scapa Flow would yet become inexorably linked with the German High Seas Fleet, and this end game would shortly be played out. Under the terms of the Armistice, the enemy surface fleet of seventy-four ships was to surrender to the Royal Navy and be interned at Scapa Flow. By 27 November 1918, the German Commander-in-Chief, Rear-Admiral Ludwig von Reuter had gathered his fleet together in the Flow, and over the months that followed, many thousands of German sailors were repatriated, leaving caretaker crews aboard each ship. For these disconsolate and unhappy men left behind, a difficult time lay ahead: they were not allowed ashore and contact with both islanders and British seamen was forbidden.

By June the following year, Germany's fate, including that of Reuter's fleet, was being decided by the victorious Allies at the Versailles Peace Conference. On 17 June, Reuter issued the following signal to his captains:

> It is my intention to scuttle the ships only if the enemy should attempt to place himself in possession of them without the consent of our Government. Should our Government concur with the surrender of our ships in the peace conditions, then the ships will be given up, to the lasting shame of those who put us in this position.

As it transpired, the peace terms were devastating for Germany and, consequently, on Midsummer Day 1919, Reuter signaled from the cruiser *Emden* that scuttling would begin at 10.30 a.m. At 12.16 p.m. the first German ship, the battleship *Friedrich der Grosse,* turned turtle and sank beneath the Flow. The Grand Fleet was out of the anchorage on exercise, and by the time it returned, just three hours later, few German ships remained afloat; by teatime the pride of Kaiser Wilhelm's navy lay on the bottom of Scapa Flow: ten battleships, five battle-cruisers, five cruisers and thirty-two destroyers. Nine German sailors were shot during the operation, the rest, defiant to the end, became prisoners ashore.

On 28 June 1919, the Versailles Peace Treaty, which would have catastrophic and far-reaching consequences for the whole world, was finally signed, and three months later, the Royal Navy closed its headquarters in Kirkwall, the Orkney capital. In February 1920, with Germany apparently reduced forever as a military power, Scapa Flow resumed peacetime status, albeit still remaining an important base for the Royal Navy.

At Versailles, the Allies intended to prevent Germany rising again as a military power. The German army was limited to just 100,000

15. Admiral von Reuter.

volunteers (officers and men), there were to be no military aircraft or aircraft manufacture, and the production of tanks and heavy artillery was also prohibited. So far as the navy was concerned, Germany was allowed only 15,000 sailors, six old battleships, six cruisers, twelve destroyers and the same quantity of gunboats. Article 191, intended to prevent a resurgence of the U-boat menace, stopped Germany from building, acquiring or operating submarines, for any purpose, and under Article 188, all 176 surviving U-boats were to be handed over to the Royal Navy. All un-seaworthy craft, including those under construction, were to be destroyed. There were many other clauses: German territory was reduced by returning parts to France, Belgium and Denmark, creating Czechoslovakia, Hungary and Lithuania, and making Danzig a 'free city'. Austria was given independence, the Rhineland was to be occupied for fifteen years and the Saar administered separately until 1935. German colonies were to be shared amongst the Allies, and, in a final humiliation, Germany was forced to accept complete responsibility for the war and pay enormous reparations to the Allied nations.

The terms of the *Versailles Diktat,* as the Treaty was known in Germany, were harsh indeed: Germany had lost all of its colonies, an eighth of its European territory, a tenth of its European population and most of its iron and steel industry. Reparations were seen by the Germans as vindictive, the War Guilt Clause simply a lie, and the *Diktat* an imposed 'settlement' of huge injustice, an all-pervading feeling of which exploded throughout Germany. Needless to say, many of the articles were soon perverted or undermined: the *Freikorps,* for example, was an immediate response to disarmament, and there were similarly immediate but clandestine plans for rearmament. Clearly, Versailles had unwittingly sewn the seeds for the growth of fascism and nationalism in Germany between the wars; so far from ensuring that another war with Germany was impossible, the *Diktat* achieved

16. U-21, a Type IIB coastal boat built in 1935. The author's friend Helmut Maros served aboard this boat, which was scrapped in 1944. Maros was a survivor of U-977, which famously ignored the surrender order and made a successful run for Argentina in May 1945.

totally the opposite; Versailles was, to Germans of all social groups, a unique act of extremely savage vindictiveness which they vowed to one day avenge.

The League of Nations (the forerunner of our United Nations today) was also established at Versailles, although, needless to say, Germany was not welcomed as a member. That was reversed in 1925, when Germany was admitted to the League as a result of the Locarno Pact, a non-aggression treaty between Germany, France and Belgium, guaranteed by Britain and Italy. Under Locarno, the demilitarisation of the Rhineland was confirmed as permanent, and German, French and Belgian post-Versailles borders were mutually accepted. Ten years later, two years after the Nazis came to power in Germany in 1933, the *Führer,* Adolf Hitler, openly announced German rearmament: the countdown to the Second World War was now well underway.

Germany had, in fact, started to rearm even before Hitler became head of the Nazi state. From 1920 onwards, the German army was being reorganised and retrained. The new Soviet Union was sympathetic and agreed to secret training programmes and military experiments for tank and aircraft crews. Consequently, when Hitler came to power, he inherited a growing military power with an army – unlike the French, British and Americans – with no vast stocks of old weapons and equipment to use up before the commissioning of new was justified. New army tactics, involving light and medium bombers flying in support of fast-moving armour and motorised infantry, called *Blitzkrieg,* were evolved. In 1923, the *Luftwaffe* had started building clandestinely under the guise of the civil airline *Lufthansa.* Although the navy was unable to rebuild, it being impossible to build great ships and submarines in secret, German sailors too looked forward to the day when their navy would inevitably rise like a phoenix.

In April 1935, the British, French and Italian heads of government met at Stresa, in Italy, reaffirmed Locarno and condemned German rearmament. The 'Stresa Front', however, soon collapsed: in March, Hitler had already announced the formation of his new *Luftwaffe,* and, in May changed the Ministry of Defence to that of War.

Later that month, Hitler advanced specific proposals to settle the 'naval question' between Britain and Germany. In a speech decidedly friendly in tone, the *Führer* recognised the 'vital importance' to Great Britain and its empire of a dominant fleet, proclaiming that Germany had 'not the intention, or the necessity or need' to engage in naval rivalry with Britain: all Germany wanted, he claimed, was a fleet of just thirty-five per cent of the Royal Navy's tonnage. In reality, Hitler's objective was to trap the British government into an agreement which, in fact, flouted the restrictions of Versailles. Britain, without consulting the League of Nations or France and Italy, with whom the British Prime Minister had met at Stresa, agreed. At last, the vital restriction on building submarines was lifted, and Hitler was allowed five battleships, twenty-one cruisers and sixty-four destroyers. This agreement, therefore, removed every single significant naval restriction and encouraged Nazi Germany to expand her fleet as rapidly as possible.

In spite of the massive restrictions imposed by Versailles, Germany had far from abandoned interest in submarines. The *Reichsmarine* had cleverly remained in contact with veteran submariners on the pretext of completing an official history of U-boat operations during the Great War, and, amazingly, the Allies had failed to seize U-boat plans and designs. A consortium of companies that formerly built U-boats began operating behind the façade of a cover company in Holland: *N. V. Ingenieurskaantor voor Scheepssbouw* (IvS). IvS was able to offer an experienced project team, headed up by Hans Techel, formerly a senior executive at *Germaniawerft*, and *Korvettenkapitän* Ulrich Blum, a veteran U-boat commander, to existing foreign and prospective naval powers, their service covering the whole process from design to acceptance trials. IvS worked out of Kiel and later the Hague on projects for Japan, Argentina, Italy, Spain, Sweden and Turkey. In this way, Germany was able to remain at the forefront of submarine design and development without breaching the Versailles *Diktat*. The Turkish contract was significant, in fact, as German 'trials' crews remained in Turkey, opening a submarine training school, ostensibly for the Turks but which in reality provided a training base for German submariners.

17. Helmut Maros, pictured today, who eventually became a prisoner of war in the UK, married an English girl and became a British citizen.

18. U-27, a Type VIIA, which was larger and more powerful than the earlier coastal boats. The Type VII, with various improvements and additions, remained the workhorse of the *U-bootwaffe* throughout the war.

The German Navy, such as it was, concealed its U-boat force as an *Ubootabwehrschule* (anti-submarine warfare school), which opened at Kiel in 1933. The following year an order was placed with *Deutsche Werke Kiel AG,* for six Type IIA coastal submarines of just 250 tons. With utmost secrecy, parts were collated and assembled, together with torpedoes from various sources. In 1934, *Germaniawerft* was given an order for ten Type IIBs, and so it went on. On 25 March 1935, four, larger, Type VIIAs were ordered. As we have seen, by May 1935, Hitler had blatantly and overtly assigned the hated *Diktat* to the rubbish bin; on 12 December 1938, the Germans advised Britain that the tonnage of the 129 U-boats now on charge equalled the tonnage of the Royal Navy's submarine fleet.

Within the small German navy between the wars was an officer widely recognised as a rising star: Karl Dönitz. Born in 1891, the young Dönitz entered the Imperial Navy in 1910, serving first as a signals officer on cruisers. In 1916, he retrained as a submariner, receiving command of his own U-boat the following year. In 1918, he was captured and held captive in Britain before returning to the German navy in 1919. Four years later, he was posted to the U-boat Inspectorate and, in 1924, moved to Naval High Command in Berlin as a liaison officer with the army. After further sea service, he returned to Berlin and another staff appointment in 1930. For the first few months of Hitler's Chancellorship, Dönitz was abroad, but he returned to a Germany of which he entirely approved. The following year, he was given command of the cruiser *Emden,* which he took on a flag-waving world cruise. Upon return, this ambitious and very capable officer fully expected to go to a bigger and even more prestigious ship before becoming a cruiser squadron commander. Destiny, however, had other plans: on 1 October 1935, Dönitz took command of the first U-Flotilla. It is widely believed that Dönitz was specifically selected to be responsible for pre-war submarine development, but this is actually incorrect. When given this appointment, which from a career perspective after the *Emden* could be considered a retrogressive step, his brief was only to make his flotilla an effective fighting force. The training and selection of personnel was not within his remit, and even his own flotilla's training school was not his but the Torpedo Inspectorate's responsibility. Indeed, other subjects relating to submarines were dealt with by the Supreme Naval Command's U-boat Office, with which Dönitz had little contact. Without set parameters, however, he was able to start building the basics of his own personal vision: the day when Germany would have 300 U-boats, operating in 'Wolf Packs', and able to successfully blockade Britain and force a surrender.

In the same way that many air force chiefs and politicians in Britain between the wars misunderstood the true role and value of fighter aircraft, so too were German admirals at High Command confused regarding the best employment of U-boats. It was first thought that U-boats should be used as meteorological stations or as escorts to surface ships – the latter a completely impractical notion given that surface raiders tended to break out during storms – when U-boats were unable to operate on the surface! By 1939, Dönitz was enthusiastically and vigorously promoting visionary strategies for submarine warfare, and published a book on the subject. Much more than a textbook, however, this clearly reflected his exalted mood of Nazi militarism and his fanatical dedication to the camaraderie of submariners. Throughout this period, Dönitz campaigned for a crash U-boat building programme. Incredibly, it was not until the summer of 1940, when the Second World War was almost a year old, that Dönitz's arguments were accepted and his U-boats were engaged as an autonomous force against British merchant shipping – with devastating results.

Germany's defeat in the Great War and the subsequent *Diktat* humiliation were injustices regarding which Dönitz, the veteran submarine commander and patriot, seethed with anger. The surrender of the German High Seas Fleet and subsequent scuttle were also considered great insults to German national pride. Scapa Flow, the scene of this drama and home of the hated Grand Fleet, was a painful thorn in the side of every German naval officer longing for revenge.

Having begun openly rearming in 1935, Hitler set about preparing for and pushing the world towards another war. In 1936, his troops reoccupied the Rhineland, and the German *Kondor* Legion was sent to fight for the fascist General Franco in Spain. In 1938, Hitler himself became Minister of War and Commander-in-Chief of the German armed forces, and the forbidden union with Austria – the *Anschluss* – went ahead in March that year. In September, the Munich Crisis loomed, Hitler effectively playing brinkmanship whilst the Allies mollified him with a weak policy of appeasement, resulting in Britain and France betraying Czechoslovakia and giving the Sudetenland to Germany. Incredibly, in August 1939, Stalin and Hitler signed the Soviet-German Non-Aggression Pact, and finally, on 1 September 1939, Nazi Germany invaded Poland. This time, the Allies had no choice: Hitler ignored their demands that his troops withdraw, so consequently, on Sunday 3 September 1939, Britain and France declared war on Germany. The world was at war for the second time that century.

The German military welcomed the war against Britain and France, which provided an opportunity for them to avenge the injustices of Versailles and establish a new order in Europe, dominated and led by Germany. For Karl Dönitz and those of his ilk, now that this dangerous peace was at last over, their time had come.

2
'The Boldest of Bold Enterprises'

Within days of the outbreak of the Second World War, *Kommodore* Dönitz began planning what he would later describe in his memoirs as 'the boldest of bold enterprises': getting a U-boat into Scapa Flow, the most important British anchorage, to wreak havoc with the Royal Navy's Home Fleet.

Dönitz knew how safe the British felt at Scapa Flow, given the security precautions taken with anti-submarine nets, blockships, minefields, booms, guardships, patrols and searchlights. This could also be to his advantage, however, as such confidence bred complacency. But, with the loss of Henning and Emsmann still very much in mind, how could a U-boat penetrate those defences? Dönitz ordered his staff to collate every scrap of intelligence possible to facilitate the attack. By the end of that first month of war in 1939, the *Luftwaffe* provided detailed aerial photographs of Scapa Flow, from which Dönitz was able to study the defences. Seven entrances could be seen: an eastern approach through Holm Sound accessed three, Kirk, Skerry and East Weddel Sounds, and Water Sound was a separate 'gate'. Hoxa and Switha Sound lay to the south, but were both protected by booms, as was Hoy Sound to the north-west. From these photographs, it was clear that a U-boat could only enter the Flow from the east, where there was a tight route between the blockships in Kirk Sound. Dönitz later wrote that 'there is a narrow channel about 50 feet wide and 23 feet deep.

To the north of the block ships is another, smaller, gap. The shore on both sides is practically uninhabited. I think that it would be possible to penetrate here – at night, on the surface and at slack water. The main difficulties will be navigational.' To strike a blow at the Royal Navy within that safest of bases, Dönitz knew, would be a great coup, shattering British morale. Weather experts advised that the best time for such an attack would, appropriately, be on the night of Friday 13 October 1939, as both periods of slack water (when incoming and outgoing tides meet) occurred during a night lit by a full moon.

Whilst U-boat Command planned their audacious sortie on 17 September 1939, the Royal Navy suffered a demoralising loss: the aircraft carrier HMS *Courageous* was sunk by U-29; 518 British seamen were lost. The loss of this capital ship was, in fact, unnecessary and reflects the confusion regarding how best to combat the U-boat threat. Churchill, then First Sea Lord, required aggressive pro-activity against the German submarines, forming 'Hunter Killer Groups' to locate and destroy them using the new ASDIC radar and depth charges. Foolishly, however, these units included not only destroyers and other anti-submarine craft but also capital ships. The latter, of course, presented huge and slow targets, a fact taken full advantage of by U-29 that fateful day. As *Courageous* went down, it was perfectly clear that, as in the Great War, the U-boat was a menace to be reckoned with.

To carry out the attack on Scapa Flow, the obvious choice of weapon was a Type VIIB U-boat. The Type VII was the mainstay of the *U-Bootwaffe* throughout the war, and the 'B' variant the most advanced at that time. With a length of 66.5 metres, a MAN diesel engine capable of 17.2 knots surfaced whilst an electric motor provided 17.8 knots whilst submerged. Travelling on the surface at 12 knots, a Type VIIB's range was 6,500 nautical miles, and submerged at 4 knots could cover 90 nautical miles. Four torpedo tubes faced forward, one aft, and nine extra 'eels' (as torpedoes were nicknamed) were carried. An 8.8 cm gun was positioned on the deck forward of the conning tower, and a 2 cm cannon provided anti-aircraft defence.

19. The Great War U-boat veteran commander and submarine warfare exponent Karl Dönitz.

20. The *Führer*, Adolf Hitler, inspects U-7, a Type IIB, before the Second World War broke out, but by which time the Versailles *Diktat* was dead and buried.

21. A U-boat Type VIIB, identical to U-47.

22. The commander of U-47, chosen by Dönitz to undertake the audacious sortie to Scapa Flow: *Kapitänleutnant* Günther Prien.

It took a crew of forty-four men to operate a Type VIIB, who lived in an almost intolerably cramped and damp environment. But which of his Type VIIBs and commanders would *Kommodore* Dönitz choose for this most dangerous of missions? There was one man cut from the same cloth as the *Kommodore* himself: *Kapitänleutnant* Günther Prien, commander of U-47.

The son of a judge, Prien was born in Osterfeld in January 1908 and, by 1939, had spent half his thirty-one years at sea. In the early days he served on schooners and trade ships, joining the *Reichsmarine* in 1933. After a year aboard the light cruiser *Königsberg,* he transferred to U-boats and was commissioned. In 1938, Prien was on U-26, patrolling Spanish waters during the Civil War. When war was declared on 3 September 1939, *Kaleun* Prien was commanding U-47 and on patrol in the Bay of Biscay; there he soon chalked up three successes, all British merchant ships: *Bosnia, Rio Claro* and *Gartavon* all went to the bottom at the hands of U-47. Dönitz concluded that Prien 'possessed all the personal qualities and professional ability required'.

Prien's later memoir was essentially 'ghosted' by a propaganda writer and, as will be seen, is clearly and significantly at odds with the facts and evidence in certain regards. However, the description of how Prien came to be given the Scapa Flow mission can, I think, be considered accurate, and is worth quoting:

After dinner we stood about chatting in the Mess of our depot ship. An orderly opened the door and *Kapitän* von Friedeburg entered. 'Gentlemen, your attention please. *Korvettenkapitän* Sobe and *Kapitänleutnants* Wellmer and Prien are requested to report to the CO U-boats.' He saluted and left.

We looked at each other and my CO asked me, 'What on earth is going on? What have you been up to? Have you been in a brawl or something?' He looked first at Wellmer and then at me. Wellmer answered for both of us: 'No, sir'. Ten minutes later we boarded a barge which was secured alongside and went over to the *Weichsel.* The harbour was peacefully quiet and we were silent too.

I considered what the CO could want with us, for such a command is most unusual on a Sunday. My companions were also lost in thought.

When we arrived on the *Weichsel* the crew of a U-boat paraded on the Tirpitz Mole; the *Kommodore* was inspecting them. We went into the Mess and waited. The minutes seemed like hours, until finally a runner came. Clicking his heels he said, 'Will the *Kapitäns* please go to the CO of the U-boats in the Admiral's Mess.'

Sobe went first and was followed by Wellmer. I remained alone and slipping up to the window gazed outside. What on earth was coming now, I wondered? The thought was becoming unbearable.

At last the runner returned. 'Will *Kaleun* Prien please go to the CO.' The runner preceded me up a few stairs and then I entered the large room. In the centre stood a large table covered in charts. Behind it stood the CO, Wellmer and Sobe.

'Beg to report present.'

'Thank you, Prien'. The CO shook my hand. 'Now please listen carefully to Wellmer', he said, and, turning to Wellmer, 'Wellmer, will you please begin from the beginning again.' Wellmer stepped up to the table and bent over the charts.

'The usual security measures are the same as always. The particular security measures which I reported in the war diary are at these points.' He placed his finger several places on the charts.

I followed him with my eyes. He was pointing at the Orkneys and in the centre of the charts was written in large letters *Bay of Scapa Flow*.

Wellmer explained further, but at that moment I could hardly follow him, for my thoughts were milling around the name Scapa Flow. *Kommodore* Dönitz, the U-boat CO, who was in the group, said 'During the Great War the British defence booms lay here.' He leaned over the chart and indicated the places with the point of a compass. 'In all probability they will be there again. In this place Emsmann was destroyed.' The compass point rested on Hoxa Sound. 'And here,' a stroke with the compass, 'are the usual anchorages of the British Fleet. All seven inlets to the bay will be boomed and well guarded. All the

23. The next four snapshots are from the personal album of U-boat commander Herbert Bruninghaus. This shows a torpedo being carefully winched aboard a Type VII.

24. U-boat men guide the torpedo into their boat's magazine.

same, I think that a resolute commander could get through just here.' The point of the compass wandered over the chart. 'Mind you, it won't be an easy job because between the islands the current is very strong. All the same, I believe that it can be done.'

He raised his head and gazed at me searchingly under lowered brows. 'What is your opinion, Prien?' I stared at the chart, but before I could answer the CO continued, 'I don't want your answer now; think the matter over carefully, take all available information with you and study your chances. I shall expect your decision on Tuesday.' I straightened up and he looked me in the eye: 'I hope you have understood me, Prien. You are perfectly free to make your own decision. If you come to the conclusion that the undertaking is impossible, you will report that fact to me.' He continued emphatically, 'No blame whatsoever will be attached to you, Prien, because we know that your decision will be based on your own honest conviction.' He shook me by the hand; I gathered up the charts and notes, saluted and left. I had myself taken out to the depot ship *Hamburg*. I locked the charts and notes away in a steel safe and then I went home.

On the way soldiers and sailors saluted me but I returned their salutes mechanically. I felt a tremendous tension within me. Would it be possible to bring it off? My common sense calculated and questioned the chances, but my will had already decided that it could be brought off. At home, supper was already on the table. Absentmindedly I greeted my wife and child, for my thoughts were obsessed with the single idea of Scapa Flow. After supper I begged my wife to go out alone, for I still had work to do. 'Oh yes, your next patrol'. But she left without further comment or question, for she was a soldier's daughter.

As soon as she had left, I returned to the depot ship *Hamburg*. I fetched the charts from the safe and took them home with me. Then I sat down at my desk and spread the charts and plans out before me. I worked through the whole thing like a mathematical problem. The care with which the defences had been planned was amazing. By the time I had finished it was already dark. Bunching the papers together I took them back to the *Hamburg*, through the dark and silent town. Only the stars glowed clear in the sky.

Next morning I requested an interview with *Kapitän* von Friedeburg. He received me at once. 'Well,' he said, looking at me through narrowed eyes, 'what do you think, Prien?'

'When may I report to the CO, sir?'

'So you are going?'

'Yes sir.'

He dropped heavily into his chair and reached for the telephone. 'I thought you might', he said, 'Only I wasn't sure on account of your wife and child.' Then he spoke on the telephone, 'Yes sir, Prien is with me now ... very good sir ... at 1400 hours, sir.' He stood up. 'Two o'clock

Above and below: 25 & 26. Remarkable photographs, snapped from a German destroyer, of a U-boat's sky periscope whilst on manoeuvres in the Baltic.

this afternoon you may see the CO' he said. 'The big lion is waiting', he added.

Punctually at two I was there. As I entered I found him at his desk. 'Beg to report present, sir', I said. He did not acknowledge my salute; it seemed as if he hadn't noticed it. He was looking at me fixedly and asked 'Yes or no?'

'Yes sir.' The shadow of a smile flitted across his face. Then, seriously again, he asked 'Have you thoroughly considered the whole business? Did you think of Emsmann and Henning?'

'Yes sir', I replied.

'Very well, get your boat ready', he said, 'We will fix the departure time later on'. He got up, walked round the desk and shook my hand. He said nothing but his handshake was firm.

We left on 8 October, at 10 o'clock in the morning. It was again a beautiful clear Sunday. *Kapitän* von Friedeburg stood on the pier with the adjutant of the Chief of the Flotilla. For a short while I stood with them on the wall, looking over to the little boat, which was made fast to the stakes. The crew were already on board.

We were walking up and down the pier, hardly saying a word. Only right at the end von Friedeburg said 'Well, Prien, whatever happens you are sure of many thousands of tons, and now, best of luck my boy.' I saluted and walked across the gangway to the boat.

The ropes were cast off and the roar of the diesels thundered through the boat. Then we were slowly making our way for the green sea, our course nor'nor'west and our objective Scapa Flow.

And so it was that in the autumn of 1939, sudden and violent death stalked beneath the North Sea, towards the peaceful Orkneys.

3

An Unhappy Ship

Confident that Scapa Flow was safe from submarine or surface attack, the Home Fleet's main fear was being struck from the air. German reconnaissance bombers operating from Norway were regularly over the Orkneys, photographing and studying the anchorage, but, as we have seen, this was not necessarily with an air attack in mind. All of this invaluable information was being fed to *Kommodore* Dönitz, who was planning the impossible: to penetrate the Orkney defences with a U-boat which, once within the Flow, would wreak havoc upon the Home Fleet.

On 26 September 1939, the Home Fleet, including such capital ships as *Nelson, Rodney, Hood, Renown* and *Ark Royal,* left the Orkneys and forayed across the North Sea; during the return trip, Ju 88 dive-bombers of KG 30, operating from Westerland/Sylt, pounced. *Leutnant* Storp achieved a direct hit on HMS *Hood,* but his bomb bounced off the ship into the sea without causing any damage. *Gefreiter* Francke recorded a near miss alongside the aircraft carrier HMS *Ark Royal,* although the German propaganda machine soon whirred into action and announced that the great ship had been sunk. Having the whole Home Fleet concentrated together at anchor in Scapa Flow, however, clearly made easy targets for the *Luftwaffe,* a fact the Commander-in-Chief, Admiral Sir Charles Forbes, was acutely aware of.

27. HMS *Royal Oak* in 1939, shortly before being sunk at anchor in Scapa Flow. Of great interest in this photograph is the starboard torpedo blister, a recently added modification which actually contributed to the aged battleship's tragic fate. (Orkney Library).

On 8 October, the German Fleet Commander, Admiral Hermann Bohm, made a clever sortie up the Norwegian coast towards the Utsire Light with his flagship, the *Gneisenau,* the cruiser *Koln,* and nine destroyers. Bohm's intention was two-fold: firstly to provide a diversion for the pocket battleships *Graf Spee* and *Deutschland,* heading for the South Atlantic, and secondly to entice the Home Fleet out of Scapa Flow to be attacked by a large force of *Luftwaffe* bombers. The enemy ships were spotted by an RAF Lockheed Hudson reconnaissance aircraft, and the Admiralty decided that the *Gneisenau* was attempting to break out into the Atlantic and must therefore be stopped. Admiral Forbes was ordered to give chase and engage, his Humber Force subsequently sailing from Rosyth, and the Home Fleet from Scapa Flow. Ironically, this diversionary enterprise by Bohm, who was unaware that U-47 was leaving Kiel that day, bound for Scapa Flow on the 'boldest of bold enterprises', would ultimately rob Prien of the rich pickings he expected to find.

28. A superb study of HMS *Royal Oak*'s forward gun turrets and bridge, the sailors on deck providing a sense of proportion. (Orkney Library).

The *Gneisenau* diversion was actually unsuccessful for all involved, on both sides. RAF Wellington bombers were dispatched to attack the enemy fleet, but failed to find it, and likewise the *Luftwaffe* missed the Home Fleet (in spite of flying 148 sorties). The Germans did bomb the lesser Humber Force, but without success, and the four U-boats briefed to take part made no contact whatsoever. Bohm managed to pass safely undetected through the Kattegat back to Kiel, and on 9 October, Forbes ordered both his Humber Force and Home Fleet back to Scotland.

With the spectre of air attack at the forefront of his mind, Admiral Forbes returned Humber Force to the Forth, but decided against returning the Home Fleet to Scapa Flow. Instead, and most wisely as indicated by subsequent events, Forbes dispersed his ships: HMS *Hood*, HMS *Nelson* and HMS *Rodney* were sent to Loch Ewe on the west coast, whilst HMS *Sheffield* stayed at sea. Only HMS *Royal Oak* (a battleship), HMS *Repulse* (a battle cruiser), HMS *Furious* (an old aircraft carrier), HMS *Newcastle* and HMS *Aurora* (both cruisers) returned to Scapa Flow. First to arrive was HMS *Royal Oak,* at 0705 hrs on 11 October, the venerable old warrior taking station in the north-east corner of the anchorage, her guns therefore able to offer anti-aircraft protection to both Kirkwall and the radar station at nearby Netherburton. The following afternoon, a *Luftwaffe* reconnaissance flight identified a total of sixty-three naval ships at Scapa Flow, this information being fed to Dönitz, who therefore fully expected U-47, scheduled to attack the next night, to find many targets. After that German aircraft passed overhead and took those final photographs. Before Prien's attack, however, nine vessels sailed from Scapa Flow, most importantly HMS *Repulse,* which went to Rosyth. Throughout the day on Friday 13 October, and as usual, Scapa Flow saw ships come and go. At 1520 hrs, the Royal Navy's latest and largest cruiser, HMS *Belfast,* anchored off Flotta, in the main area of the Flow. HMS *Royal Oak,* however, remained in the north-east corner, together with the twenty-five-year-old aircraft carrier HMS *Pegasus,* and just 1,000 yards offshore.

29. HMS *Royal Oak* lying at anchor in Scapa Flow, starboard view. (Orkney Library).

30. HMS *Royal Oak* at full steam and turning at speed in the Pentland Firth. (Orkney Library).

31. HMS *Royal Oak* wreathed in gunsmoke during practice firing in the Pentland Firth. (Orkney Library).

By the outbreak of the Second World War, however, HMS *Royal Oak* was far from the pride of the Royal Navy. One of five *Royal Sovereign*-class battleships, *Royal Oak,* costing just under £2.5 million, had been built between 1914-16, at Devonport dockyard, the largest and final such ship to be constructed there. *Royal Oak* was armed with eight 15-inch guns (in four turrets), twelve of 6-inch calibre and eight 4-inch anti-aircraft guns. In addition the battleship boasted four 21-inch torpedo tubes. She weighed 29,000 tons, 40,000 bhp engines achieved a top speed of 20 knots, and her full compliment was over 1,000 men. Powered by four Parsons turbines and eighteen oil-fired boilers, that vital area of the ship was protected by armour plate thirteen inches thick. So heavy was this, however, that it could only extend five feet below the waterline, and the minimal number of doors and hatches along this belt of thick steel could only be opened mechanically.

In 1934, armour plate four inches thick was added to the main deck, protecting magazines and machinery below, but this weight negatively affected the ship's reserve buoyancy and stability. Below the waterline, in 1922, fourteen-foot-long anti-torpedo blisters had been added, the idea being that a torpedo would spend its force rending open the hollow blister, leaving the hull either unscathed or with only minimal damage. These blisters added even more extra weight, reducing the ship's performance further still.

In 1916, HMS *Royal Oak* had fought at the Battle of Jutland (although, having only joined the Grand Fleet two weeks previously, was not considered fully operational), at which she was credited with two hits, an impressive achievement for a newly commissioned ship. By 1939, this still proud but now old battleship was obsolete, this fact having become abundantly clear during the *Gneisenau* patrol. During that foray across the North Sea, the weather was awful, and *Royal Oak* had been unable to keep up with the Home Fleet. It seemed that the ship's future lay in static harbour anti-aircraft defence, or perhaps bombardment, or as a 'long stop' in the complex manoeuvres required to head off German warships (such as the *Gneisenau* patrol, from which the *Royal Oak* had just returned).

Bert Pocock remembers:

> I joined the *Royal Oak* at Portsmouth in June 1939. We sailed to Weymouth where I was a member of the party detailed to collect the Royal Family's baggage from the local station and convey it to the Royal Yacht. *Royal Oak* then sailed to Scapa Flow. I was a Boy 1st Class, and I thought it was great to be in the Royal Navy; little did I know what dark days there were ahead.
>
> At Scapa Flow we anchored in Kirkwall Bay, and were there when war was declared on Germany, 3 September 1939. A big cheer went up from the crew, boy, were we going to show 'em! The officers were called together by the Captain, W. H. Benn, and drank the toast 'Damnation to the enemy'. Then the First Lord of the Admiralty, Winston Churchill himself, came aboard and spoke to us. It was inspiring.

Then we were sent out on patrol. The sea was really rough, there was six inches of water splashing around the Boys' Mess Deck, as a result of which it was only possible to sleep on the tables and benches there. So, it was good to get back into Kirkwall Bay and have a run ashore for a couple of days.

Another Boy, of which there were many aboard *Royal Oak*, was Arthur Smith:

I was just sixteen years old when, on 1 June 1938, I walked through the gates of HMS *St Vincent*, a boys' training establishment, to begin ten months of hard work, hard, but fair, discipline, and a thorough grounding in the workings of the senior service. March 1939, saw me, together with my classmates, joining HMS *Hawkins*, a cruiser of the Reserve Fleet tied up in Portsmouth Harbour and one of only two ships in the Royal Navy armed with 7.5-inch guns (the other being HMS *Frobisher)*. There we became conversant with every aspect of shipboard life, with the exception of watch-keeping (a pleasure yet to come!). I enjoyed my time aboard this ship as there was a slight lessening of the rigid discipline, and the opportunity to have a (duty-free) cigarette without the fear of eighteen cuts across the backside with a cane was bliss. I really began to feel like a sailor. However, all good things come to an end, and in June of 1939, together with 200 other Boys, I was drafted to HMS *Royal Oak*, to form part of the ship's company. This was again in Portsmouth.

I was now seventeen and about to experience five and a half months of misery. I am afraid to say that *Royal Oak* was not a happy ship, especially for Boy Seamen. Some ships are happy, others not; it was hard to put your finger on why she was an unhappy ship, but unhappy she certainly was. Luckily it was my only experience of this kind. Anyone who has not experienced the difference between a happy and unhappy ship cannot begin to imagine the effect that this atmosphere can have on shipboard life.

When war was declared, my Action Station was in the 'A' Turret Shell-Room, which meant that I only did four-hour watches at sea and

32. HMS *Royal Oak*, port view. (Orkney Library).

enjoyed all night in my hammock whilst in harbour. However, on Sunday 8 October, on my way to the NAAFI to buy a bar of chocolate, I was passing the Gunnery Office when I was called by the Chief Gunner's Mate, who demanded to know where my Action Station was. When I told him 'A' Shell-Room, he replied 'Not any more, it is now S1 four inch AA gun. One of the gun's crew is in Sick Bay with appendicitis, and you are his replacement'. I cursed my luck at this, as AA crews kept watch in harbour, which obviously meant losing my all night in.

At that time I was unaware that this unexpected turn of events whilst going to get a bar of chocolate would be instrumental in saving my life a few days later.

Ken Toop was also a Boy 1st Class, who had likewise been through training at HMS *St Vincent* and HMS *Hawkins*:

When one joins a ship, the choice of hammock-slinging hooks is limited because the first ones to join sling wherever they choose. Boys, for obvious reasons, are required to sling in the Boys' Mess Deck, under the watchful eye of the Boys' Instructor and PTI. But because there were more bodies than hooks on HMS *Royal Oak*, I had to find a hook elsewhere, which was in the Port Six Inch Gun No. 2 working space. In the next hammock to mine was a Boy called McCarthy.

Again, Ken's forced alternative sleeping arrangements would soon play an unexpected part in saving his life.

On the night of Friday 13 October 1939, the crew of HMS *Royal Oak* settled into their bunks and hammocks, having re-provisioned and cleaned up the mess caused by heavy seas during the *Gneisenau* patrol. Safe at anchor within impregnable Scapa Flow, the ship's company, excepting the few on watch, gratefully settled down to sleep.

4

The Gates of Hell

When U-47 left Kiel, only the *Kaleun,* Günther Prien, knew that the boat's destination was Scapa Flow. His crew were puzzled as the smoke trails of ships beyond the horizon were not investigated, as the boat ploughed on nor'nor'west. Gradually, the weather worsened, the barometer fell and a gale began – the same storm that was simultaneously making life uncomfortable for HMS *Royal Oak* on the *Gneisenau* patrol. U-boats were designed to travel mostly on the surface, using their powerful diesel engines, submerging only to avoid detection and sometimes attack (so in reality these were more accurately 'diving boats' rather than submarines). As U-47 fought the gale, those on watch, swathed in oilskins but still drenched by the cold North Sea, eventually, through the darkness, saw the shadow of land. Prien's second-in-command, *Oberleutnant* Englebert Endrass asked his captain if they were to 'visit the Orkneys?' Prien's response was 'We are going to Scapa Flow', which would have shaken a lesser man. Endrass simply replied, 'That will be OK, sir, that will be quite OK.'

On 12 October, U-47 lay submerged during the day, just off the Orkneys, surfacing during the evening and approaching the coast to fix the boat's exact position. At 0437 hrs on Friday 13 October, U-47 gently settled on the seabed, 90 metres below the surface, just off the Orkneys. It was then that Prien decided to tell his crew of their mission.

33. Engelbert Endrass, Prien's second in command on U-47. He later commanded his own boat, becoming a highly decorated *Kaleun*, but was lost with all hands on U-567, north-east of the Azores, on 21 December 1941.

Assembling the men in the Forrard Mess, the news was greeted with absolute silence. Prien (as he later wrote in his memoir) issued instructions:

> Everyone except the watch will go to their bunks and sleep, the watch will wake the cook at 1400 hrs. At 1600 hrs we will have dinner. Then for the duration of the mission there will be no more hot food. Only cold sandwiches at all stations. And everyone will have a slab of chocolate. All superfluous light will be extinguished, we must economise on electricity; no one is to move unnecessarily, for we shall be lying aground for this evening and must be careful with the air. During the mission there is to be absolute silence. No message is to be repeated.

Dismissed, the crew of U-47 went to their bunks. Prien tried, but was unable to sleep. In the Ward Room he found his navigator, Spahr, pouring over his charts, before returning to his bunk and sleeping until 1400 hrs, when the Watch went to wake the cook, creeping past the *Kaleun*'s

34. Boy 1st Class Bert Pocock, a 'Reading townie'.

35. Captain William Benn, captain of HMS *Royal Oak*.

bunk with his feet wrapped in cloth so as to ensure perfect silence. At 1600 hrs, as per Prien's orders, the crew was wakened and enjoyed a substantial hot meal of veal cutlets and green cabbage. Tables were then cleared and charges fixed with which to scuttle the boat should the mission fail and U-47 fall into enemy hands. Prien reiterated his instructions: during the entire action smoking and unnecessary talking were forbidden. Lifejackets were checked. Two 'eels' were placed in the rapid loading position before tubes one and two. In the boat's log, Prien noted that the crew's morale was 'splendid'.

At 1900 hrs, U-47 surfaced to periscope depth. Prien scanned the area, confirming it was safe. At 1915 hrs, the grey submarine slid from beneath the waves and surfaced. The conning tower hatch was opened, allowing fresh air to rush in, and Prien, two officers and his Bo'sun quickly scrambled up onto the open bridge, clad in cumbersome oilskins. The wind had dropped; the swell was much reduced, and all around was clear of the enemy. Fans were started to ventilate the boat, electric motors stopped and diesel engines started. Prien set course for Holm Sound: there was no turning back now.

At 2307 hrs, just before Rose Ness, U-47 sighted an unidentified merchant ship and dived, remaining submerged until 2331 hrs when the boat surfaced in Holm Sound, the entrance to Kirk and Skerry Sounds. So close to land, U-47's diesel engines were too noisy, so Prien switched over to the much stealthier electric motors. Cloud cover was light, the night bright and clear, and across the entire horizon danced the Northern Lights, something that the planners had not anticipated. In Skerry Sound, Prien could clearly see the blockship there, and, as a result, wrongly believed that he was in Kirk Sound. Spahr, using dead reckoning, contested the boat's presumed position, and Prien soon realised his mistake. Altering course hard to starboard, collision was avoided, and just a few minutes later, Kirk Sound was clearly visible.

In his boat's log, Prien wrote:

It is a very eerie sight. On land everything is dark, high in the sky are the flickering Northern Lights, so that the Bay, surrounded by highish mountains, is directly lit from above. The blockships lie in the Sound, as ghostly as the wings of a theatre.

Prien's conscientious and thorough study of his charts now paid off. Deciding to pass through on the northern side of the blockships, following a course of 270, U-47 passed the first one with 315 metres to spare. Then a strong current hit the boat from starboard, simultaneously Prien spotting the cable of the northernmost blockship, the *Soriano,* lying at an angle of 45 degrees ahead. With port engine stopped, starboard engine slow ahead, and rudder hard to port, the tricky current was negotiated, although the U-boat scraped along the bottom and its stern caught the cable. Slowly the boat eased free, and, turning to port and with some 'difficult rapid maneuvering', resumed course. A combination of tide and electric-motor power then swept U-47 into St Mary's Bay; Prien had achieved the impossible: U-47

36. Boy 1st Class Kenneth Toop. 37. Able Seaman Stanley Cole.

was now safely within Scapa Flow and still undetected. Quite simply, the *Kaleun* announced, 'We are inside'. At that point, however, the whole mission was nearly scuppered: as the boat passed the village of St Mary's, just half a mile away, the headlights of a car suddenly illuminated U-47. Fortunately for Prien, no alarm was raised and the car turned and continued towards Kirkwall.

In U-47's all-important log, Prien recorded that at 0027 hrs on Saturday 14 October, 'It is disgustingly light. The whole Bay is lit up. To the south of Cava there is nothing. I go farther in. To port, I recognize the Hoxa Sound coastguard, to which, in the next few minutes, the boat must present itself as a target. In that event, all would be lost; at present south of Cava no ships are to be seen, although visibility is extremely good'.

Finding no targets to the south, Prien turned U-47 north, creeping along the coast. The log records that, at 0055 hrs, 'Two battleships are lying there at anchor, and, further inshore, destroyers. Cruisers

38. Alf Fordham pictured today.

39. Royal Marines Musician Alf Fordham.

not visible, therefore attack on the big fellows. Distance apart 3,000 metres'. Prien had found the old battleship HMS *Royal Oak*, bows to the north-east, and the ancient aircraft carrier HMS *Pegasus*, slumbering peacefully in the north-east corner of Scapa Flow and in the lee of Kirkwall's cliffs. The excitement felt by Prien and those with him on U-47's bridge can only be imagined; later, Prien wrote:

At last, over there ... close to the shore appeared the mighty silhouette of a battleship. Hard and clear, as if painted into the sky with black ink. The bridge, the mighty funnel and aft, like filigree, the tall mast. Slowly we edged closer. At such a moment all feeling stopped. One became part of the boat, the brain of this steel animal which was creeping up towards its enormous prey. At such a time you must think in iron and steel-or perish.

40. The drifter *Daisy II*, for the skipper and crew of which no praise could be too high in respect of their efforts to save *Royal Oak* survivors.

41. HMS *Royal Oak* was hit by four torpedoes, this being the propulsion unit of one, recovered by divers and proving beyond doubt that the battleship had been sunk by a U-boat. This artefact can be seen today in Stromness Museum, Orkney.

42. U-47 returns to Wilhelmshaven and a hero's welcome.

43. U-47 cheered by German sailors as the boat enters port.

In the heat of the moment, however, the old aircraft carrier *Pegasus* was identified as HMS *Repulse,* a most desirable target, although because of its position, *Royal Oak* would have to be attacked first. The 'eels' were made ready.

As U-47 turned to starboard, at around 0100 hrs, Endrass gave the order for all four forward torpedo tubes to fire. One 'eel' jammed, the other three sped towards their target. Spahr counted down the seconds to impact: 20, 15, 10, 5. Turning around, Prien fired his stern tube. Some four minutes later, a single explosion was heard (it being suspected that the *Repulse* had been hit), but to those watching from the bridge of U-47, *Royal Oak* appeared unaffected. Still on the surface and aware that detection was doubtless imminent, Prien fired another three torpedoes from the bow. Prien describes the consequent destruction:

Now something occurred that no one had anticipated and no one who had seen it would ever forget. A wall of water shot up towards the sky. It was as if the sea suddenly stood up on end. Loud explosions came one after the other like drumfire in a battle and coalesced into one mighty ear-splitting crash. Flames shot skyward, blue … yellow … red.

Behind this hellish firework display the sky disappeared completely. Like huge birds, black shadows soared through the flames, fell hissing and splashing into the water. Fountains yards high sprang up where they had fallen, huge fragments of the mast and funnels. We must have hit the ammunition magazine and the deadly cargo had torn the body of its own ship apart.

I could not take my eyes from the glass. It was as if the gates of hell had suddenly been torn open and I was looking into the flaming furnace. I glanced down into my boat. Down there it was dark and still. I could hear the hum of the motors. Spahr's even voice and the answers of the planesman. I felt as never before my kinship with these men below who did their duty silently and blindly, who could neither see the day nor the target, and died in the dark if it had to be. I called down, 'He's finished!' For a moment there was silence.

Then a mighty roar went through the boat, an almost bestial roar in which the pent-up tension of the past twenty-four hours found release.

At 0014 hrs, Prien's first torpedo had hit the starboard bow of HMS *Royal Oak*, one plate below the waterline, the resulting explosion tearing a hole 40-50 feet wide and three plates deep. Captain Benn was advised that the most likely explanation was merely an internal explosion in the ship's inflammable store. That a torpedo was responsible was not even a consideration. Arthur Smith, however, remembers:

At midnight I took up position on S1 four inch on the Four Inch Gun Deck for the middle watch, 0000-0400 hrs, to be told that I was to make my way up to the starboard wing of the bridge, where I would perform the duty of aircraft lookout. The night being as black as it was, I didn't fancy my chances of seeing any if they did fly over, but orders are orders so up I went. I remember thinking how cold it was, when the ship literally jumped to a massive explosion, directly below me on the starboard side. A column of water shot up, whilst the port anchor chain ran out, the cable roaring across the fo'csle unchecked and making an incredible noise. It didn't take a genius to work out that we had been torpedoed, but how could that be? We were in Scapa Flow, a secure anchorage; little did we know how insecure it really was until much later. Action Stations was piped, so I ran down to the Four Inch Gun Deck to join my gun's crew. There was considerable speculation as to the cause of the explosion, and when I said that we'd been torpedoed I got a clip around the ear from the captain of the gun crew and told not to be such an idiot, and only speak when spoken to! Talk about boys should be seen but not heard! After about fifteen minutes, Fall Out from Action Stations was piped, the majority of the ship's company hopping back into their hammocks whilst I was sent back up to my lookout position.

44. *Kaleun* Prien on his bridge – his immaculate uniform suggests that this is a posed shot.

Bert Pocock:

Just after midnight there was an almighty bang, which I felt good and proper as my hammock was up against the side of a ladder. Being on the short side this meant I was able to climb up the ladder and step into my hammock, instead of having to swing in. It was this that saved my life. With that bang, all we Boys jumped out of our hammocks, wondering what had happened. A Chief Petty Officer came running through on his way forward and told us to get back in our hammocks, so back in our hammocks we went. At least fifty hammocks were slung in the Boys' After Mess Deck, very crowded by today's standards. I looked across to my three fellow Reading townies and gave a smile with thumbs up. Then things quietened down a bit.

Alf Fordham was a Musician in the Royal Marines, having joined as a 'Band Boy' in 1933 when just fourteen-and-a-half. He had served on HMS *Royal Oak* since 1937:

I was asleep in my hammock when I and many others were woken by a noise, and the ship shuddered. Nobody knew what had occurred; no one would have thought it was a torpedo in harbour. I stayed in my hammock, which probably saved my life. I saw the Gunnery Officer pass by, looking very worried. Then through the tannoy 'Take magazine temperatures', which sounded very worrying.

Ken Toop:

After 'Pipe Down', the ship's passages below deck are lit by lights low down on the bulkhead. When the first torpedo struck, forward on the starboard side, I was asleep and did not hear it. McCarthy got up and went to investigate, returning saying, 'You'd better get out, Lofty, something's happened.' So I hurriedly got my trousers and shoes on, which was, fortunately as it turned out, protection for my back and feet. I attempted to climb the Midship Companion Way, as the emergency lights were still on, but there were a lot of chaps all with the same idea, so I made my way forward through the screen door.

Whilst a certain amount of concern and confusion swept through the ship, many sailors, below decks and in their hammocks, went back to sleep, dismissing the interruption as an internal problem and not particularly serious. Others, like Toop and McCarthy, felt uneasy and made their way on deck.

Those watching from the bridge of U-47 were confused as to why the two other forward-firing torpedoes, and the one from astern, had not exploded. Unbeknown to them, their electrical torpedoes at that early stage of the war were unreliable, sometimes running too deep, or erratically, on occasion exploding too soon, sometimes too late. Having reloaded the three operational bow tubes, Prien fired a salvo of three more 'eels' at *Royal Oak*. This time, the effect was catastrophic.

Arthur Smith:

Hardly had I resumed my position as aircraft lookout than the ship rocked to three more explosions, again from the starboard side. Almost immediately, the ship listed to starboard and I was pretty sure that she was finished. When the order to 'Abandon Ship' was piped, I immediately ran down to the Four Inch Gun Deck, which I intended to jump off, and one of my most vivid memories of that night was struggling to release the toggles of my duffel coat with cold fingers. By the time this was accomplished, there was no time left to divest myself of boots and uniform, so into the sea I went, fully clothed.

Alf Fordham:

About ten minutes after being awakened came the most violent explosion which seemed to lift the ship out of the water. We all jumped out of our hammocks.

45. The crew of U-47 travelling to their audience with the *Führer* in Berlin. Thousands of cheering people lined the route in an incredible display of appreciation.

46. U-47 had expunged the shame of 1919, and the population of Berlin were clearly determined to demonstrate their approval.

Bert Pocock:

About ten minutes after the first bang, there was another, bigger bang that nearly threw me out of my hammock. Out went the lights, and you could feel the ship starting to list starboard. Chief or no Chief, I knew there was trouble, so with the ladder alongside of me, it was up and through the escape/hatch (as the big main hatch was down because the ship was only on standby), which only one man could pass through at a time. As I went through the hatch, I lined myself up for the next ladder heading up to the Galley Deck. I then started to move forward with my arms out and moving my legs around to feel anything, as it seemed darker than dark. I said to myself, 'Mum, help me out of this one!' It seemed like a lifetime but I caught hold of the ladder and you could still feel the deck going over. As I was going up the ladder I called out, 'Anybody there?' but the only sound to be heard was a loud hissing. I was hopeful that there was an answer, as I was scared going up alone in the darkness. I knew that the next ladder was only a yard away on the Galley Deck, and that this led out into the night, which was fairly dark. I had to go on all fours to the ship's side, working towards the bows, going slowly into the sea, as they say you can get sucked back into the ship when going down. Once in the sea, I swam like mad away from the ship.

Ken Toop:

The ship was starting to list to starboard, so much so that I was able to leave over the port side, sliding down and stepping on the slight ledge where the anti-torpedo blisters joined the ship's side. By clambering and crawling, I managed to make my way aft along the side towards the stern, where the drifter, *Daisy*, attached to the ship as a tender whilst in harbour, was tied up alongside – but by this time the ship was turning over onto its starboard side and so the *Daisy* had to be cast off, or she would have floundered. I was left with no option but to move up the side towards the keel, until sliding into the sea was unavoidable. I entered into a thick covering of oil fuel on a freezing sea.

Pocock and Toop were lucky to escape. The first torpedo of this second salvo hit *Royal Oak* roughly amidships and below the Boys' Mess Deck, killing and maiming many of the young sailors in their hammocks there. Indeed, it was this explosion that had nearly thrown Pocock from his hammock. Following that explosion the ship came alive, men all over jumping from their hammocks, but then there was another hit, this time further aft on the starboard side; a hole was torn in the armoured deck and killed many men in the Stokers' Mess Deck. When the electricity supply subsequently failed, the ship was plunged into darkness, accentuating the panic and chaos below decks. Without power, it was impossible for orders to be transmitted over the tannoy, or to send a distress signal. As *Royal Oak* listed, water poured in through portholes, the glass having been removed and replaced with ventilators whilst the crew was at anchor. The seawater rushing into the ship increased the chaos and suffering within, and hastened the ship's instability.

Then the 'hellish firework display' described by Prien started. Alf Fordham:

> I stopped to put my trousers on, that delay saving my life: had I run forward immediately, in an effort to gain the Quarter Deck, I would have run into the most intensely hot orange flame, which shot through the door; because I had stood still, it missed me by a few feet. A cordite magazine had exploded and vented wherever it could.

Had Fordham run into that white-hot flame, it would have cremated him on the spot, sadly the fate of many sailors. Everything inflammable touched by that blowtorch went up in flames. He continues:

> Seeing this I reversed my direction. Because the lights were out, it was pitch dark. A group of us tried to open the door leading aft through the officers' quarters, but I couldn't get the cleats off properly in the dark. After a minute or two, Musician 'Ned' Kelly – bless him – shouted 'Stand back, stand back' and methodically went around the many cleats and successfully got the door open, through which many men poured.
>
> I reached the Quarter Deck and dimly through the darkness saw

dozens of men attempting to get on *Daisy,* the drifter tied alongside. After a few minutes I suddenly realised that the deck was listing beneath my feet, so I ran to the stern, intending to jump off, but didn't make it. Suddenly I slipped down some distance and hit the water, going down miles it seemed. As I surfaced, something touched my back and I thought the ship was coming down on top of me, so I did a very fast swim away. It was so dark that I had not seen the ship going over to starboard, nor seen her sink. The water was extremely cold and I was covered in thick oil.

On the tender *Daisy II,* a quick-thinking crewman, Johnnie Duthie, saved her from going under by cutting the rope holding her to the doomed battleship, which sank below Scapa Flow in less than ten minutes. With the sea around him covered in thick black oil and screaming men, the tender's skipper, John Gatt, suddenly found himself directing a major rescue operation.

Able Seaman Stanley Cole was amongst those men in the water:

I could smell the oil-fuel, but could not avoid getting some in the mouth, nose and ears; I kept my eyes closed until I surfaced. Coughing and spluttering, I became aware that my right foot and leg seemed to be hanging in the water as I began to swim away from the ship's side, along with some others. It was like trying to swim through liquid tar, and I was convinced that I wasn't going to make it.

The water was bitterly cold, and from all around me in the darkness I could hear cries for help from injured, burned and despairing bodies. Kicking out as best I could with my good leg, I was sure that I could feel the bodies of drowned shipmates under my foot. Then my hand caught something, a piece of wood about 2 feet long by 6 inches wide, so I hung on to it in the blind faith that it would keep me afloat – I would have killed anyone who tried to take it from me! Then another stroke of luck: what I took to be a five gallon oil drum came within range and I tried to hold my arm over it, as it slipped and rolled with the oil. Finally, after what seemed like ages, I made out three or four bobbing heads paddling slowly along a length of timber, which I suppose could have been one

47. Adolf Hitler awards Prien the coveted *Ritterkreuz*, the Knight's Cross of the Iron Cross.

of the 'deals' we adapted for seating at church services etc. I let go of the drum but not my small scrap of wood, and joined up with the lads paddling the deal. We tried shouting and singing, our throats hoarse, but without success, growing colder and more exhausted. One of our number slipped off the plank and we never saw him again.

My last view *of Royal Oak* was of her keel, silhouetted against the dark skyline. She appeared to have turned right over. Then, just as I had all but given up the struggle, along came a ship's whaler and I felt myself hauled over the boat's side, with two or three other lads dumped on top of me in a cold, sodden, oily heap.

Whilst the individual bodies were being taken from the water, the crew of the drifter *Daisy II*, under the command of skipper John Gatt, were valiantly picking men up until *Daisy* herself was in danger of capsizing under the sheer weight of numbers.

Ken Toop:

Once in the sea I managed to take off my shoes and trousers, which had saved me from barnacle cuts off the ship's bottom, which I had slid down into the water. I was not a strong swimmer, having only met the Royal Navy's minimum standard (three lengths of the open air baths at HMS *St Vincent* and staying afloat for three minutes in a canvas duck suit). Nothing, though, prepares one for the oil-fuel-covered winter coldness of Scapa Flow, but eventually I managed to bump into a catamaran, a hefty wooden frame which was hoisted over the side by the crane when the ship was riding alongside a jetty, so I managed to climb onto it; two other half-dead men were already on it.

We floated around for I don't know how long, and the *Daisy* eventually picked us up. There were oil-covered bodies everywhere. Some had to be put down into the fish hold, others lying round the funnel. The skipper made his way over to HMS *Pegasus,* where we spent the night trying to clean the fuel off us, which was impossible with only hard soap: no shampoo or detergents back then.

Bert Pocock:

I started to swim for the shore, as I felt more at ease out in the open, and I was a very good swimmer. Then I saw the trawler *Daisy* and went after it. By the time I was pulled aboard they said that *Royal Oak* had gone under. I shed a few tears, knowing that my fellow Reading townies had no chance of getting out.

Gatt's crew of six, Orkney fishermen all, rescued 360 men from those freezing oily waters, but were grief stricken as they had to pull away and heard the cries of 'Don't leave us *Daisy*' from doomed sailors left in the water.

Arthur Smith:

When I went into the sea, the ship's launch, a large boat, was still tied up to the starboard boom, so I climbed aboard with quite a few others. By this time, though, *Royal Oak* had listed at an angle preventing us from releasing the launch from the boom, as the painter was like an iron ball. I came to the conclusion that things were becoming rather dangerous, so, once again, I took to the sea. By this time the ship was going over rapidly, and I decided that the sooner I departed the scene the safer I would be. I hadn't gone far when she turned turtle, displacing a large wave which grabbed me, turning me over and over and down. I was totally helpless, but thankfully didn't panic, and kept kicking out in the hope of reaching the surface, which eventually I did, but not before taking in a couple of breaths of water which was most unpleasant. How I blessed my old dad at that moment for chucking me in the deep end of the local swimming baths when I was five years old and teaching me to swim.

Suddenly all the yelling, screaming and explosions stopped, and a deathly silence reined. I knew that she had gone. I did not know, of course, how many hundreds of my shipmates had gone with her, which in retrospect was probably a good thing. I tried floating on my back for a while, until I heard voices not too far off. Swimming over to investigate I found a carley life raft which was rather overloaded, so, with what I suppose was the optimism of youth, I decided to go solo; another reason was my dislike of the officer sitting on the raft issuing orders!

Remembering that when I went on watch, shore side was to starboard, and having jumped over on the starboard side, I struck out in the direction I was facing, believing that I would eventually hit land. Wrong! Striking out strongly with what we used to call the side stroke, I headed for the middle of Scapa Flow – away from shore! Ignorant of this fact, I felt faintly confident that in time I would set foot on dry land, as I was young and strong and supremely fit having boxed and played football to a high standard. As I was swimming alone I heard splashing and came upon another lad whose navigation had proved as bad as mine. Having established identities (he was also ex-*St Vincent* and *Hawkins)* we concentrated on our swimming in silence, when he suddenly said 'Oh bollocks to this' and disappeared under the water. I think that scared me more than anything that had gone on before, to think that a young seventeen-year-old could give up the ghost with no fuss or commotion. Poor lad had just reached the end of his tether.

48. Hitler joins the crew of U-47 for lunch at the *Reich* Chancellery.

Time stood still for me then and I was very cold, my boots weighed a ton and proved impossible to remove, due to the slimy coating of fuel-oil. The clothing was no problem, and maybe helped keep some warmth in my body. Although still swimming my strength was rapidly deserting me. I probably started to hallucinate, seeing my mother and knowing how she would react if I was to die. This probably gave me the incentive to carry on to the bitter end. Even so, I'd just about had it when I heard a voice say 'Here's another one', and I was grabbed and hauled into a boat, manned, by all people, four men of the RAF! It transpired that they were crewmen from the *Pegasus,* an old Great War catapult ship. When they heard the explosions they launched a boat and investigated. They saved three or four of us and I am truly glad that I had the strength left to thank them when they put us aboard their ship, where I was taken to a boiler room, my uniform and boots cut off and, standing in that lovely warm place, washed down with paraffin and cotton waste, given a blanket and a tot of rum which, combined with my exertions, knocked me right out.

According to Prien's memoir, which becomes unreliable at this point, written as it was to be a morale-boosting piece of propaganda, after the final three explosions the anchorage then sprang into action, U-47 immediately changing from hunter to hunted. This was actually far from the truth, as there was no reaction from the defenders. Survivor Arthur Smith comments:

> Over the years since I have read many books and articles by people who claim to have been at Scapa Flow on the night of 13/14 October 1939, in which they describe destroyers dashing about dropping depth-charges, guns being fired, and searchlights illuminating the scene. Prien said that the Northern Lights were evident; well, I saw and heard none of it, and I am neither deaf nor blind.

In his log, Prien justified his decision to withdraw at that point given that his periscope did not permit him to conduct submerged attacks at night, he could not be expected to manoeuvre unseen any longer on the surface, and in any case, he was sure that the driver of the car at St Mary's had seen, and therefore gone to report, U-47; moreover, he believed that further north within the anchorage lay unseen destroyers.

With both engines running at high speed, U-47 withdrew. At Skildaenoy Point, low tide and current worked against Prien, as again indicated by the boat's log:

> I must leave by the south, through the narrows, because of the depth of water. Things are again difficult. Course 058, slow – 10 knots. I make no progress. At high I pass the southern blockship with nothing to spare. The helmsman does magnificently. High speed ahead both, finally 3/4 speed full ahead all out. Free of the blockships – ahead a mole! Hard over and again about, and at 0215 hrs we are once more outside. A pity that only one was destroyed. The torpedo misses, I explain, are due to faults of course, speed and drift. In tube 4, a misfire. The crew behaved splendidly throughout the operation.

To his crew, Prien announced: 'All stations. Attention. One battleship destroyed, one battleship damaged – and we are through!'

The relief amongst U-47's crew must have been unimaginable. With five torpedoes left, Prien set course for base.

Behind him, Prien had left death, destruction and misery. HMS *Royal Oak* lay 32 metres beneath Scapa Flow, and 833 of her crew were lost with her. The survivors were grateful to be alive, but in shock.

Ken Toop:

Having spent what was left of that fateful night aboard *Pegasus*, the next day we were taken over to the battleship HMS *Iron Duke*, lying off Lyness, to have reports taken from us regarding our position on the *Royal Oak* and how we escaped. The next day we were taken by ferry to Scrabster, on the mainland, and by bus to Thurso. There we were put into civilian houses for a couple of days until we travelled by train to Portsmouth in our survivors' outfits. It took weeks to get the oil-fuel out of our hair and off our bodies, especially those that had the misfortune to swallow some. We were then sent on survivors' leave within a day or so, no way of letting our poor parents know any details, just a brief letter from Thurso confirming that we were alive and an announcement in the *Sunday Graphic* with a list of survivors, and that was it, we arrived home with a few shillings pay. Boys' pay was eight shillings and ninepence a week, but we all came from poor families; I had two small sisters and a father who was sixty. He had lost an eye when only seven, but still served in the army during the Great War. So, at the end of ten days survivors' leave it was back to the dockyard at Portsmouth to join the cruiser HMS *Manchester* – shortly to leave for Scapa to spend the winter in Icelandic waters and on Northern Patrol until the Norwegian campaign started.

According to my records, the number of Boy Seamen, Boy Telegraphists and Boy Signalmen aboard HMS *Royal Oak* was 163. Only thirty-seven were saved. In spite of reports to the contrary, I still say that the ship sank in just a little over seven minutes.

Having also been rescued by *Daisy II,* Alf Fordham recalls the aftermath:

> Aboard HMS *Pegasus* we were given, with much kindness, rum, cocoa, a bath and clean clothes. The next morning we were taken to the SS *Voltaire* to await transport south. Then another unexpected experience. We were lying off Lyness and experienced our first air raid. The old battleship *Iron Duke,* being used as a depot ship, was damaged. We were very nervous on the *Voltaire,* a huge liner – it seemed such a good target.
>
> Later we were taken by train to Thurso and joined our train to go south. During the night's journey we were awakened by a bang and the carriage shook violently. A goods train was being shunted onto the same line – fortunately we were both moving slowly so no one was hurt.
>
> 'What was left of our Royal Marines band, ten survivors out of fifteen musicians, arrived at Deal. We were kitted out with new uniforms and sent on survivors' leave.

Bert Pocock:

> The night before we left by train for Portsmouth, we were put up by residents in Kirkwall. They were extremely kind to us, a lovely lot of people. I subsequently served on HMS *Manchester,* on which I could not have had a worse action station: the Telephone Exchange, right down in the bottom of the ship with hatch slammed down and clamped from outside. When we went into action we prayed that we did not get hit because we could not get out. Of the thirty-seven Boys who survived the *Royal Oak,* only eighteen, including myself, saw the war through.

Arthur Smith:

> The following day we boarded the *Voltaire,* which was brought to life and became home for a few days, during which time we were subjected to a bombing raid which left us unscathed but damaged HMS *Iron Duke,* a recent arrival.

Almost as traumatic was the Board of Inquiry. There I sat, a seventeen-year-old boy seaman facing more senior officers than I ever thought existed. They put me at ease immediately and were so kind and sympathetic you wouldn't believe. I suppose it was all the gold braid that initially made me nervous. Shortly after this we were taken to the town of Thurso where we were treated like royalty. I cannot speak highly enough of those wonderful people who gave so much and asked for nothing in return. After a few days we boarded a train at Thurso Station, bound for Portsmouth, which we reached over thirty hours later – what a journey! We did, however, enjoy a wonderful breakfast in Perth and a good late meal in London. Upon arrival at Royal Naval Barracks, Portsmouth, we had a cold meal and a packet of ten cigarettes each – and there were more than 400 of us. Next on the agenda was a really good sleep, after which we were re-kitted and sent on fourteen days survivors' leave.

For U-47, those few days after the attack were spent returning to base, running on the surface at night and lying stationary on the bottom at ~~night~~ DAYTIME. During the long hours of waiting before their attack, a comic had circulated amongst Prien's crew, the men being particularly amused by the drawing of a bull charging an invisible target with lowered horns and steaming nostrils. When nearly home, Endrass called for a brush and white paint, reproducing the drawing on the conning tower's side: so it was that Prien would become known as the 'Bull of Scapa Flow', a symbol of aggressive spirit, an example to all Germans.

As U-47 raced homewards, the crew listened eagerly to news bulletins from the *Grossdeutsche Rundfunk*. British Admiralty reports confirmed that HMS *Royal Oak* had been sunk, 'believed by U-boat action'. As the boat approached Wilhelmshaven on 17 October, a special German broadcast announced that:

Further to earlier reports of the sinking of the British battleship HMS *Royal Oak,* it is now learnt that the commander of the U-boat, *Kapitänleutnant* Prien, penetrated the strong defences protecting the anchorage of Scapa Flow and torpedoed the ship in harbour during the night. The battleship blew up in a few seconds.

When news of Prien's success was broadcast in Germany, there was an absolute frenzy of enthusiasm throughout the Fatherland. U-47 had, effectively, expunged the humiliation of the German High Seas Fleet at Scapa Flow in 1919. U-47 was escorted into Wilhelmshaven by two destroyers and welcomed home by cheering crowds and music. Dönitz himself had travelled especially from Kiel, conferring the Iron Cross 1st Class on Prien and the 2nd Class on the rest of his crew.

U-47 soon left the lock and tied up at its permanent berth. There, an officer came aboard and handed Prien, the 'Bull of Scapa Flow', an invitation from Hitler himself for the commander and crew of U-47 to be his guests in Berlin. In the capital, the news that Prien and his U-boat heroes had been summoned for an audience with the *Führer* spread rapidly and when Prien and his men landed at Tempelhof, the airport was packed with people. The radio had announced that Prien's party would travel to the Kaiserhof Hotel, and the route was lined with hysterical crowds, tens of thousands of people, who threw flowers, cigarettes and presents into the open cars as the sailors passed. The hotel itself, where the crew of U-47 was staying, was virtually besieged, the crowd ceaselessly chanting 'We want Prien!' When the crew left the *Kaiserhof* for their audience with Hitler, the crowd actually broke through the police cordon, blocking the street and forcing the submariners to retreat and leave via a back exit.

At the Reich Chancellery, Prien paraded his crew in a large study. Although muted, the cheering crowds could still be heard. Prien himself wrote:

The adjutant entered and announced the *Führer*. He came in. I had often seen him before, but never had I felt his greatness as intensely as in this moment … But what was I in comparison with this man, who had felt the degradation of this land on his own, who had dreamed of a freer and happier Fatherland? An unknown man amongst 80 million he had dreamed then acted. His dream had come true; his acts had forged a new world.

I marched up to the *Führer*. He shook me by the hand and placed the Knight's Cross of the Iron Cross around my neck, honouring the whole crew through me. I felt pride and happiness in this hour; it would be stupid to deny it. But I knew that I stood here, representing the many who, nameless and silent, had fought the same fight ... The *Führer* walked along the short line of men, gave everyone his hand and thanked each and every one of them. I walked behind him and looked at them all, man by man, and my heart beat in unison with theirs.

Hitler then made a speech to the crew, mentioning his own experiences under fire in Flanders during the Great War, explained the full significance of their success at Scapa Flow. Prien then reported to Hitler in private before the *Führer* sat down to lunch with the whole crew, who were later taken to the Propaganda Ministry for a tea to which the German press were admitted. Then Prien was the star at a press conference to which both Allied and neutral correspondents were invited. In the evening, U-47's crew were joined at the Wintergarten Theatre by none other than Dr Joseph Goebbels, the Minister of Propaganda himself. The audience cheered, and during the interval, Prien had to make a speech. Afterwards, the crew were taken on to a nightclub where, in their honour, the ban on dancing had been lifted for that occasion. When asked by a German war correspondent for his impression of the reception in Berlin, the 'Bull of Scapa Flow' replied, 'On my arrival I became conscious for the first time of the deep interest the German people had taken in what was, for us U-boat men, a routine voyage. I am convinced that my crew has also been inspired to do everything they can to bring this war to an early, honourable and victorious end.'

Günther Prien had become the first U-boat commander of the Second World War to receive the coveted Knight's Cross, which now hung glittering from its red, white, and black neck ribbon. Whilst the mood in Germany was completely euphoric, the reverse was true of the effect of U-47's 'routine' sortie on the British.

49. The victorious Prien, now a household name throughout Germany and beyond, with his crew after the Berlin celebrations.

At stunned Scapa Flow, confusion and speculation remained rife about the sinking of HMS *Royal Oak*. Although the ship's captain, Captain William Benn, was convinced he had been torpedoed, the only way to be sure was for divers to examine the wreck. Sandy Robertson, a local commercial salvage diver, was sent for from his cottage on Hoy at 3 a.m. At daylight out in the anchorage, lying in just thirty-two metres of water, the hull of the sunken battleship could be clearly seen. Robertson's task was grim; hundreds of bodies lay scattered on the seabed, and he found three big holes in the ship's hull. Then he found the crucial piece of evidence: the propeller of one of Prien's torpedoes. Once salvaged, there was no more argument: incredible though it seemed and painful as it was to admit, the enemy had achieved the impossible and penetrated the anchorage's 'impregnable' defences with a submarine, torpedoing *Royal Oak*. Not only that, but the belligerent vessel had also escaped, completely unscathed and undetected.

The fate of *Royal Oak* was released to the British people the same day. Coming so soon after the *Courageous* disaster, it was an absolutely shattering blow to British national pride and morale – especially given that the ship had been lost within Scapa Flow. The nation just could not understand how this tragedy had happened. Most of the ship's company were from Portsmouth and Devonport, and in those areas, families were desperate for news of their loved ones; they would have to wait several days before lists of survivors were available and published accordingly.

On 17 October, the First Lord of the Admiralty, Winston Churchill, spoke in the House of Commons about the disaster. Whilst it was accepted that a U-boat was responsible, Churchill commented that it remained 'a matter of conjecture' as to how the submarine had penetrated the defences, given that, throughout the Great War, 'the anchorage had remained immune from such attack, on the account of the obstacles imposed by the currents and net barrages'. Paying tribute to Prien's feat of arms, Churchill said, 'this entry by a U-boat must be considered as a remarkable exploit of professional skill and daring.'

Although officially he described it as 'a regrettable tragedy', Churchill impressed the fact that the loss of *Royal Oak* would have no bearing on the overall war at sea. Inwardly, however, the First Sea Lord was deeply saddened by the loss *of Royal Oak*.

Naturally, a Board of Inquiry was immediately convened, which heard testimonies from numerous witnesses and went through the whole business with a very fine-tooth comb. No evidence was obtained that a submarine had either entered or left the flow, and nor was there any indication that a U-boat had been destroyed in the anchorage. The Board agreed, however, that the experience of survivors (no doubt supported by Robertson's discovery of the torpedo component) suggested that the *Royal Oak* had been hit by torpedoes, and one witness, Marine Owens, Bandmaster 2nd Class, had imparted a crucial eyewitness account:

> I went over [the side of the ship] with another person, I think an officer. He was wearing pyjamas and was very tall. After we got 300 yards from the ship we trod water to have a rest. He then said 'Hello, do you see that over there?' I looked in the direction he pointed and distinctly saw the conning tower of a submarine some 200 [sic] yards away. The submarine was on the starboard quarter of the *Royal Oak* and appeared to be stationary. After that I said to my companion we had better make for the drifter, which was lying some 400 yards to port of the *Royal Oak*. We swam towards the drifter. I then missed my companion and have been unable to trace him since. I am absolutely certain I saw the conning tower of a submarine from my position in the water. I have not the slightest doubt whatever.

Owens was considered a first-class witness and his testimony was accepted. Having confirmed that a U-boat was indeed responsible, the Board of Inquiry also considered the state of Scapa Flow's defences, which were clearly inadequate, concluding that they required 'reconsideration' to include patrol vessels, ASDIC defences, minefields, the complete blocking of the eastern entrances (where U-47 had

50. The so-called 'Churchill Barrier', constructed of concrete blocks by Italian prisoners of war, between Glim Holm and Lamb Holm. The series of barriers built between several of the islands prevented a repetition of the *Royal Oak* disaster.

sneaked through), lookouts, guns, searchlights, and the extension of boom nets as close to the seabed as was practical. In all, eleven possible weak spots were found at which a U-boat could have entered Scapa Flow – hardly an impressive scenario and one which laid blame for the tragedy firmly on the Admiralty, which naturally blamed the senior officer on the spot, Admiral Sir Wilfred French, ACOS, who was retired. This was unfair: before the war, French had warned his Commander-in-Chief that he would be willing to take a destroyer, much less a submarine, through Kirk Sound in the right conditions; no heed was taken of this warning. Blaming French was clearly an extremely unjust decision, and probably a political one.

A sub-committee was set up to research the defensive situation, concluding that blockships were insufficient to seal off the entrances to Scapa Flow. Instead, it was decided to construct concrete causeways, called 'Churchill Barriers', between the islands concerned. In due course these were built by Italian prisoners of war, who also left behind a somewhat more artistic cultural legacy: a superb chapel built in a prefabricated hut on Lamb Holm (and which can be visited today). Although the barriers were not entirely completed until 1944, the Germans never tried to venture within the lion's den again.

What Prien's victory did do for the *Kriegsmarine* was not only to exorcise the ghosts of the Kaiser's navy's defeat in 1918 and the consequent 'Grand Scuttle' in 1919, but to increase Hitler's confidence in the *U-bootwaffe*. Indeed, straightaway the *Führer* lifted the existing restrictions on U-boat operations: all enemy ships, including liners in convoy, would be attacked on sight. For the first time, the whole nation embraced the idea that the hated Royal Navy could be defeated. As a result of Prien's success, Dönitz was promoted to Rear-Admiral and Commander-in-Chief of U-boats. He had proved the worth of the submarine, and was now in a position to actually put his 'Wolf Pack' theories into practice. As Churchill, who later became Prime Minister of wartime Britain, wrote after the war, 'It was only the U-boat menace that ever really worried me.'

5
Hearts of Oak

The suffering of those trapped inside the sinking HMS *Royal Oak* can only be imagined, and their sacrifice should never be forgotten, 833 men who are now but names on a casualty list. But in life they were much more than that, real people, alive and vibrant, with hopes, aspirations, and families. Some were mere boys, others mature men with wives and children. The loss of all was tragic. All these years later, it is impossible to trace the families of them all, to collate a documentary and pictorial record of those who died, but I have been able to obtain such details from a number of relatives who lost loved ones that fateful night in Scapa Flow, and these sailors now represent the kind of men that made up the ship's company of HMS *Royal Oak*. Their likeness and memory, through this book, will, I hope, live on, as a symbol of what mankind lost not only on the night of 13/14 October 1939, but equally throughout the entire war. It has often been said that 'their like will not be seen again'; current world events suggest that there remain sufficiently patriotic men and woman to fight for freedom and democracy, but society today has changed enormously from the days when U-47 torpedoed *Royal Oak*. The men and boys that follow in these pages, therefore, are reminders of a bygone age, one more innocent, perhaps, than today, but one which saw the world engulfed in flames.

When researching a record such as this, there can be no set

parameters: some families have masses of information, photographs and documents having been carefully preserved over the years, others have little or nothing. With that in mind, what follows in respect of each casualty has been provided by their families, who, whether they have a box of mementoes or just a faded, crumpled, snapshot, still feel this loss keenly, reflecting with great pride upon the fact that their ancestor served in the Royal Navy during World War Two, and, indeed, went down with the 'Mighty Oak'.

Finally, before we see these lost souls once more, the reader should reflect upon these words from Psalm 107, 23-24:

They that go down to the sea in ships,
& occupy their business in great waters;
These men see the works of the Lord,
And his wonders of the deep.

BOY 1ST CLASS FRANCIS WILLIAM ANNELL

As if to underline how difficult research into wartime casualties can be these days, all we have relating to this seventeen-year-old is a photograph from survivor Bert Pocock and the scantest of details: Boy Annell, the foster son of Fred and Elsie Cole of Caversham, Oxon, remains 'missing' and is remembered on the Portsmouth Naval Memorial at Southsea. That imposing tribute commemorates 24,888 seamen who gave their lives during both world wars, 14,922 of them during the Second World War and who have no known grave. This memorial was erected after the Great War, then extended after 1945, the architect being Sir Edward Maufe also likewise designed the memorial to 'missing' British and Commonwealth airmen at Runnymede. Those whose names are inscribed on the Southsea monument were associated with Portsmouth naval base, the other two manning ports at Chatham and Plymouth having their own memorials. Every October, the HMS *Royal Oak* Association holds a moving service of remembrance at Southsea, attended by survivors and the relatives of casualties, after

51. Boy 1st Class Francis William Annell. (Bert Pocock).

52. Boy 1st Class Roland Arno. (Doris Leek).

which a get together is held at HMS *Excellent*. The service is taken by the Rev Ron Patterson MBE, who served on HMS *Hood* between the wars, and the whole event organised by survivor Kenneth Toop. It was at Southsea in 2004, with my son James and friend Elwyn Harper, that I was able to meet both survivors and casualties' relatives and considerably progress my research.

BOY 1ST CLASS ROLAND ARNO

Roland Arno was also seventeen, the son of William and Hannah Arno, and hailed from Sunderland, County Durham. Like Annell, he has no known grave and is remembered on the Southsea Memorial.

PETTY OFFICER HENRY GEORGE ATTFIELD

Now just another name at Southsea, Petty Officer Attfield, a Boys' Instructor, joined HMS *Royal Oak* on 1 June 1939, and was forty-six when he perished:

> When we lost our father, my sister, Evelyn, was nine months and I was eight years old. We lived in Victoria Street, Portsmouth, with our mother, Alice.
>
> On 14 October 1939, I was standing outside the furniture shop Jays, with Evelyn in the pram, whilst my mother paid a bill inside. I heard a passing postman say that the *Royal Oak* had been sunk, so we rushed home to hear the news confirmed on the radio. My uncle, Arthur Attfield, was in Portsmouth at the time (he was killed on HMS *Cossack* two years later), and scanned the lists of survivors on the dockyard gate, but had no luck. Later my mother received a letter written by my father, date stamped 14 October, with one for me enclosed, which I still have.
>
> After watching Portsmouth Guildhall burn during the blitz, my mother, sister and I moved out into the country, to East Meon in Hampshire, where, in order to be housed, Mum had to take on three small girl evacuees. The property had a thatched roof, no running water,

electricity, gas or sanitation. Although still at junior school I was the eldest child in the house so had lots of man's jobs to do.

The evacuees' Uncle Roy worked in Portsmouth Dockyard, regularly visited the children, and in 1944, married my mother. He was a very good man, died in 1980, my mother in 1995.

My father was born in London one of eight children, the youngest of which, Aunt Flo, is still alive, aged ninety-three and has celebrated seventy years of marriage. She has told me much about my father, who was apparently into gymnastics with his brother, Arthur. I still use a couple of tools that once belonged to Dad, which, apart from his medals and a few photographs, is pretty much all I have to remember him by.

In 1947, I joined the Royal Navy, aged sixteen years. My first ship was HMS *Glasgow*, my father served thereon when it was launched; I had my photograph taken in the same position he had before me.

SUPPLY ASSISTANT ARTHUR EDWARD BARGERY

Another name on Southsea, Bargery's sister, Mrs Margaret Warburton, shares with us memories of her long-lost brother:

Arthur was born on 9 July 1919, and was just twenty when he died; I was nine years younger than him. Of course I was very proud of my big brother and missed him when he joined the Royal Navy in 1938. My friends all thought he was very dishy (1938 word!) when he came home in uniform. Arthur was a very gentle person and many of his friends were surprised when he joined up, but to get a job in the professions, if you did not have money, was difficult, and Arthur thought he would get ahead quicker in the Royal Navy. He loved it, and his letters were always cheerful and interesting.

Music was Arthur's big love and he played the piano very well. I sang all the popular songs and he encouraged me. On Saturday 14 October 1939, we received a letter from the ship, posted on the Friday morning, but unbeknown to us *Royal Oak* had already been sunk by then. In his letter, Arthur asked me to save him the song sheet from the *News of the*

World newspaper, so this, of course, became a poignant memory.

Our father was at work on the fateful Saturday morning, but as he left to come home someone called out to him 'I hear they have sunk a battleship, the *Royal Oak*.' Dad came home in a terrible state to discover that we already knew, as a special edition of the *South Wales Echo* had been printed, which I had gone out and bought; this was, of course, a terrible way for us to hear.

Friends from all over Cardiff came to visit and as we had no telephones, they got on buses or walked, bringing cake or flowers, but especially love and support. I don't remember going to bed, but I know the next morning my mother went to church as Dad and I poured over the lists of survivors. As time went on, Dad told me that he feared hope was fading away. At 4 p.m. on the Sunday, the Telegram Boy came with the news that Arthur was missing. Tributes came from people he once worked with, the schools he had attended and, of course, his peers, many of whom were also to perish during the war. My parents were always very proud of him and had faith that Arthur's life was not sacrificed in vain.

ABLE SEAMAN HAROLD BROWN

Like Annell and Arno, we have a photograph but little else: Brown was twenty-one, the son of Ellen Brown of Derby and is remembered on the Southsea Memorial.

LEADING STOKER WILLIAM EDWARD CHESMAN

Having previously served on HMS *Vernon*, Chesman was twenty-seven when he went down with *Royal Oak*. On 2 April 1938, he had married Barbara Joan Adams, the couple subsequently having two sons, Peter William and Edward Charles. Again, Chesman's name is recorded on the Southsea Memorial.

SUPPLY ASSISTANT HUBERT JOHN COUSINS

An unmarried twenty-year-old, the son of Walter and Rose Cousins of Havant, Hampshire. His cousin, Ralph, has preserved the last letter Hubert wrote to his father from HMS *Royal Oak*:

> I played football against the Royal Marines, we beat them 4-3 and a very good game it was. The RNVR who played for us took the team's photo, so later I will send you one if you would like ... There are plenty of buzzes going around the ship, but nothing official yet about leave. Xmas will soon be here and the weather is getting colder every day. I have been writing this in a special corner of my own, but now Jimmy is doing the rounds, so I will close. We have rounds at 20.30 instead of 21.00, to enable us to listen to the news. It's a very quiet war up to now. I sincerely hope that we finish him quick. Have you seen 'Old Moore's'? It gives hope.

As Ralph says, Hubert's remark about it being a 'quiet war' up at Scapa Flow proved tragically ironic. Cousins is remembered at Southsea.

CHIEF STOKER ERNEST WILLIAM FARR

Aged thirty-eight, Farr had previously served on HMS *Hood*, the great ship famously sunk by the *Bismarck* in 1941. Married to Elizabeth and from Southampton, Ernest Farr was a father with a young son, Gordon, and his name appears on the Southsea Memorial.

BOY 1ST CLASS HARRY GRIFFIN

Mrs Joan Hathaway remembers her brother:

> Harry was born on 2 June 1923, the third of six children and the eldest son, having two elder sisters, the first born of which dying at eight months. We lived in Walsall, Staffordshire. Our father was killed in a

mining accident in January 1937.

Harry was a good son and a kind and loving brother. He was a Patrol Leader in the Scouts, which is where he saw the sea and ships. It became his great ambition to join the navy and see the world. He went to HMS *Ganges* training ship when only fifteen. Harry sent mother a telegram to say that he was on his way to join HMS *Royal Oak* at Portsmouth on 2 May 1939. Shortly afterwards mother received a letter from Harry saying what a wonderful ship *Royal Oak* was, and saying how much he was looking forward to her visiting the ship on Navy Day. That would have been August 1939, but it was cancelled due to threat of war. Another brother, George, also joined the Royal Navy at sixteen; he went all through the war on Russian convoys and then submarines, serving for sixteen years altogether.

Harry Griffin is yet another name on the Southsea Memorial.

BANDMASTER (ROYAL MARINES) ARTHUR JAMES GOLDING

Aged thirty-five, Arthur Golding's name is likewise on the Southsea Memorial, but his story is particularly moving, as described by his nephew, Brian Otway:

My aunt, Mrs Dorothy Golding, was reunited with her husband Arthur on 14 October 2000, when her ashes were carried by her grandson, Christopher Meikle-Kilford, and lovingly placed inside the wreck of the *Royal Oak*. This moving act of remembrance reunited Christopher's grandparents sixty-one years to the day after the attack on HMS *Royal Oak*, in which Arthur Golding perished.

As a young boy being brought up in Cornwall, I simply accepted that all the ladies in my immediate family, my two aunts and my mother, were single parents. It wasn't until I was much older that I realised what a tough life they had led, for while my own mother was divorced, both my aunts were war widows having lost their husbands on HMS *Fiona* and HMS *Royal Oak*.

53. Petty Officer Henry George Attfield. (Colin Attfield).

54. Supply Assistant Arthur Edward Bargery. (Margaret Warburton).

Despite the fact that all three sisters were scattered around the United Kingdom, they regularly met up and supported each other throughout their lives. It was during her annual visits to Cornwall that I first came in touch with Aunt Dorothy. When I moved to live in London in my teenage years I became even closer to her. She then lived in Gosport, Hampshire.

Earlier in life I had always simply thought of my aunt as a lady who lived a straightforward life all on her own, but over the years I have realised that she was an exceptional and a very strong lady. With these thoughts in mind, I shall do my best to bring her the credit she deserves.

As a young girl, Aunt Dorothy (maiden name Luly) lived in Plymouth and was brought up by both her aunt and gran, at Hotham Place, Millbridge.

In 1924, aged nineteen, she met and married a Royal Marine called

Arthur Golding, aged twenty, and they set up home in St Luke's Road, Gosport. Arthur went on to become the Portsmouth Royal Marine Bandmaster, and shortly after the war broke out he was drafted with his Royal Marine Band to serve on HMS *Royal Oak*.

A few months before the fatal attack, the *Royal Oak* was fitted out with additional radar equipment at Devonport Dockyard. On route to Norway, where she was to survey German fleet movements, the *Royal Oak* moored up overnight in Portsmouth waters. This allowed some local members of the crew and ship's staff to pay a short visit to their families. Uncle Arthur took this opportunity and spent a few hours with his wife and children at their Gosport home. Arthur returned to his home that night with a head injury having suffered an accident during the trip from Devonport Dockyard. These were the last hours that Arthur spent with his family.

Shortly after the *Royal Oak* set sail for Norwegian waters, Aunt Dorothy returned home to visit her family in Plymouth. It was there on the Sunday morning that she first heard of the attack on the *Royal Oak*. Her son Keith had been playing near the Devonport Dockyard gates in Albert Road, he ran all the way home when he saw a posted news board stating that the *Royal Oak* had been sunk in the early hours of Sunday 14 October.

On returning to her home in Gosport, she was officially informed that her husband was listed as missing. Dorothy was aged thirty-five, and: widowed with two children Mavis and Keith aged fourteen and seven respectively.

Despite her tragic loss, she joined the Royal Marines and served with them until the war was over. On leaving the Royal Marines she started working at the Royal Navy training establishment at nearby *St Vincent*, where she remained until retirement as the canteen manageress. In her years at *St Vincent* she met hundreds of young sailors and, being the salt of the earth, no doubt was an inspiration to them, giving them support and encouragement throughout their training.

Throughout her life Aunt Dorothy proved to be simply wonderful and blessed with tremendous strength of character as she overcame some of life's most difficult obstacles, and she was always on hand to help her family out. These strengths were put to the test when her daughter lost her husband in a car crash in 1960, and further tested when her son and family immigrated to Australia in 1966. Every other year for the next eighteen years, she flew to Australia, once going by boat, to see her family and grandchildren. She continued to make this long journey until her late seventies, when the travelling became just too difficult.

In 1984 (aged eighty), following a long period when she supported her daughter through ill health, her strength was once again tested when her daughter sadly died, but as always Aunt Dorothy was there with her practical support to her three grandchildren.

Aunt Dorothy remained in her home at St Luke's Road, Gosport, until the mid-1980s when she decided that she could no longer live on her own. She then put into practice the advice she had always given to others. She sold her home and moved into a nursing home in nearby Fareham. She quickly became a favourite in the nursing home making lots of friends, and was known as 'Goldie'. Whenever visited by family members she was always bright and full of questions to both young and old. She loved to receive family photographs of the children which were immediately installed to the large photo frame beside her chair. This proved to be something that she loved to look at and ponder over most days. In 1999, Aunt Dorothy's strength was once again tested when she was told by the nursing staff that her son Keith, who had immigrated to Australia thirty-three years earlier, had suddenly died.

During what proved to be the final visit made by my wife and me in September of 1999, she was as always surrounded by her family photographs and letters. During this visit she recalled that one of the nurses had not completed the letter of condolence to her late son's widow and family. She directed my wife to search a drawer where we found the unfinished letter. Aunt Dorothy dictated a further letter which was promptly posted, bringing her peace of mind.

Aunt Dorothy died quite fittingly on Remembrance Day, 11 November 1999, at the age of ninety-four.

55. Able Seaman Harold Brown.

56. Leading Stoker William Edward Chesman. (Rachel Chesman).

The family thought it fitting that arrangements should be made for Aunty Dorothy's remains to be interred in the wreck of the *Royal Oak*.

I knew beyond a shadow of doubt that she would have approved of such arrangements for I recall her words and thoughts when she came to my assistance in 1975. Aunt Dorothy (then aged seventy) gave me very important help and counselling when I was suddenly widowed, and in doing so talked about her own heartbreak, of how she worried and felt disturbed with the knowledge that her beloved Arthur was at rest in a watery grave. She wished his head injury, suffered just before his final visit home, had been serious enough to put him off his ship. She was aware that her thoughts and worries were the same as hundreds of other war widows and that evening she expressed a wish to travel to Scapa Flow, to be near him. After looking at the practicalities of the trip, especially in the winter months, she changed her mind, but asked me to keep a promise, that I would visit the *Royal Oak*'s war grave site and scatter flowers for her.

I kept that promise, years later in 1994. After scattering the flowers in the sea, I gathered three pebbles off the beach and sent them to her in the Fareham nursing home, along with photographs recording the flowers being delivered to the sea. She kept those pebbles in her handbag for the rest of her life.

We were blessed with brilliant weather on the day of the service of Aunt Dorothy's internment. It was a very moving service at sea on board the salvage vessel *Salmaster*, led by the Kirkwall Minister, attended by some family members, Naval Officers and members of the Royal British Legion. Following the service, Aunt Dorothy's ashes were gently lowered to her grandson in the diving boat and taken past a Royal Navy launch. On deck were young Sea Cadets and naval divers who gave her the traditional Navy farewell salute before Christopher started his descent to the *Royal Oak*, 89 feet below, and finally passed his gran's casket into the ship via a porthole, mid-ship on the port side.

The following inscription was secured to the casket:

In Memory of Royal Marines Bandmaster Arthur J Golding
& All Those Who Perished With Him on This Ship,
HMS Royal Oak, on October 14th, 1939.
And His Wife Dorothy FMM Golding WRNS, Royal Marines, Ret'd.
Now Reunited With Him This Day, October 14th, 2000.
We Shall Remember.

Throughout the internment ceremony and the family's short visit to Kirkwall, we were made so welcome by the people. The fact that the whole ceremony event passed without a hitch was due to the precision of organisation by the Royal Navy led by Lt Cmdr David Turner, and the Royal British Legion, particularly (the sadly now late) Mr Charles Millar BEM.

The family would once again like to offer their thanks to all those involved who so ably helped us to reunite a wonderful lady with her

57. Chief Stoker Ernest William Farr. (Gordon Farr).

58. Boy 1st Class Harry Griffin. (Joan Hathaway).

beloved husband who had perished sixty-one years earlier, with special thanks to the under mentioned people and their parties: Rear Admiral B. Perowne (Chief Executive, Naval Bases & Supply Agency), Lt Cmdr David Turner (FOSNI Diving Team, Faslane Naval Base, Scotland), Mr Charles S. L. Millar BEM (Royal British legion, Kirkwall, Orkney) and Peter Rowlands (Ocean Optics Ltd).

MARINE KENNETH EDWIN HALL

The eldest son of Frank and Henrietta Hall, nineteen-year-old Marine Hall came from Reading and had five brothers. The family lived at 36 Beauchamp Road. Young Ken sang in the choir at St George's, was a Sunday school teacher and, in childhood, a member of the *Reading Chronicle*'s 'Happy Club'. After *Royal Oak* sank, the Club's 'Uncle Tim' wrote:

Uncle Tim would like to place on record the deepest sympathies of all members of the club with his relatives in their very sad loss, and ask every 'Happy' to remember him in their prayers tonight. This little thought is all one can do for one so young who died steadfast for his country, but his mother will know and, I am quite sure, cherish the thought that hundreds of little children will this very night be offering up a fervent prayer for her brave son.

A pupil at Wilson Senior School, Ken's ambition had always been to follow his father into the Royal Marines, with which elite unit Mr Hall had served on the *Glory* at Gallipoli. The date of his death, 14 October 1939, was coincidentally his grandfather's birthday.

Marine Hall is remembered at Southsea.

MARINE CHARLES FREDERICK HEMSLEY

The son of Frank and Agnes Hemsley, Charles Hemsley came from Sheffield, but his age on the day he died aboard HMS *Royal Oak* is unknown. He is remembered at Southsea.

BOY 1ST CLASS H. H. HIXON

Although Hixon's name appears amongst the list of men lost on HMS *Royal Oak*, the Commonwealth War Graves Commission appears to have no information regarding this casualty. His photograph appears courtesy of survivor Bert Pocock, but no further details are known of this sailor.

BOY 1ST CLASS JOHN FRANCIS HUMBER

Only sixteen when he was lost on *Royal Oak*, this casualty's younger brother, Paul, remembers:

Our father was a farmer, but our mother was killed in a car accident on

13 October 1935. She had been out cycling with John, and was hit by a car in Ashington, West Sussex. Previously, John's sister, Helena, had died age five, on 14 August 1935, so the 13th and 14th days of every month were unlucky for our family. Of course John's ship was lost on the night of 13/14 October 1939.

After our dear mother was killed, John looked after me in a fashion, I was just six. I must have been a burden to him, poor lad, until our father married again in 1936. Our dear stepmother booted John out when he was fourteen, so he obviously joined up to get a roof over his head.

Another name at Southsea, John Humber's epitaph is provided by his record of service, describing him as 'Very good throughout'.

PETTY OFFICER HENRY ARTHUR KERSEY

Henry Kersey joined the Royal Navy at HMS *Ganges* as a fifteen-year-old 'Boy' on 13 July 1920. His son, Mr Wally Kersey, remembers:

Our first knowledge of the sinking of HMS *Royal Oak* in Scapa Flow was on the 9 a.m. news, Saturday, 14 October 1939. My Dad's mother, who worked in a Brighton Hotel, was sent home to be with us. We were all in a great state of shock. We were also joined by our uncle, Mum's brother, who stayed with us all day, doing all he could and collecting newspapers that listed the survivors' names. Mum seemed to know that Dad had not survived; she had a dream that the worst had happened. Then, at 1.30 p.m. on Sunday, 15 October, we received the official telegram regrettably announcing our father's death.

When we lost Dad I was thirteen, my brother Pete was nine and the youngest, David, was five. I can still remember how we used to count the months, weeks and days until Dad's return from various commissions, which lasted anything up to three-and-a-half to four years away from home. This time, however, there would be no homecoming, no matter how distant. His death was a great shock, which deeply affected our Mum. She was brave, however, and somehow kept going for our sakes.

59. Bandmaster (Royal Marines) Arthur Golding (*extreme left*, in Kirkwall a few hours before HMS *Royal Oak* was sunk). (Via Brian Otway).

60. Brave lady: war widow Dorothy Golding. (Via Brian Otway).

She was faced with a big drop of income, but when she applied to the Admiralty for help all that was offered was to put the eldest son on a training ship and the other two in a naval home – this, I am pleased to say, she refused! Mum had to go out to work long hours to keep us all together, and the sacrifices she made I will never forget.

A gunner's mate, Petty Officer Kersey was thirty-four when he died, and his name can also be found at Southsea.

ORDINARY SEAMAN DOUGLAS MANWARING

This eighteen-year-old had followed his brother, William, into the Royal Navy; tragically both were lost with HMS *Royal Oak* and are remembered at Southsea. Recorded as being the son of Thomas and Clara Manwaring, the family were from Portsmouth. The only other detail known about this casualty is that he trained at HMS *Wildfire*, the shore establishment at Sheerness.

STOKER 1ST CLASS RICHARD WILLIAM MANWARING

The twenty-seven-year-old brother of Douglas Manwaring, Richard was married to Rose, of Coxhoe, County Durham. He is also remembered at Southsea.

STOKER 2ND CLASS THOMAS GEORGE OSBORNE

Mrs Kate Hooper remembers her elder brother:

Tom was nineteen when he died. I was fifteen when we heard the terrible news that HMS *Royal Oak* had been sunk; I don't remember how we heard it, probably on the radio. I remember the family standing by the back door of 108 West Street, Portchester, and my father leaving at about lunchtime to walk to Portsmouth Dockyard. In those days we could walk across open fields and so the distance was not as far as it is now by road. My father waited all that day and the next, to see if Tom's name came up on the casualty lists.

The thing I remember most about my brother was his pride in his uniform, especially the bell-bottomed trousers he wore. They had to be folded up properly so that the creases went round the legs, not from top to bottom. He used to put them under his mattress each night and sleep on them so that in the morning they were smartly creased and ready to wear. As you can see from the photograph, he was at HMS *Victory* (barracks) before being posted to *Royal Oak*, which was his first and last ship.

Tom Osborne's name is also recorded at Southsea.

ABLE SEAMAN CHARLES JOHN PALMER

Jessie Palmer, of Laindon, Essex, had five sons, the three youngest brothers all joining the Royal Navy. Charles, the first to join, went to HMS *Ganges* (Royal Navy Training Establishment, Shotley) on 15 April 1921. Leaving there on 3 October, Palmer's first ship was the old coal-burning dreadnought HMS *Monarch*. A few months later, he was posted to the battleship HMS *Conqueror*, on which he remained until the ship was decommissioned the following year. His next ship was HMS *Diomede*, a brand-new ship having only recently been completed at Barrow's Vickers Yard, and in the process of fitting out at Portsmouth. *Diomede*, a ship in the 5th Light Cruiser Squadron, then went out to the China Station for three years. Afterwards, Palmer served on other ships on both the America and West Indies, and Mediterranean Stations. In 1930, his ship HMS *Cairo* returned to 'Blighty' for refit, but for Palmer, it was back to China Station for another three years aboard HMS *Cornwall*. After that overseas tour, he served aboard two destroyers in Home Waters before joining *Royal Oak* on 7 June 1939.

On 15 October 1939, Mrs Jessie Palmer received the telegram informing her that her son had died on 'war service'.

61. Dorothy Golding's grandson, Christopher Meikle-Kefford, places his grandmother's ashes inside the wreck of HMS *Royal Oak*, reuniting her with her long-lost husband, Bandmaster Arthur Golding. (Via Brian Otway).

62. Marine Kenneth Edward Hall. (Shirley Bird).

Tragically, she would receive two more before the war was over: all of the Palmer brothers perished serving in the Royal Navy during the Second World War.

Able Seaman Palmer's age when he died is unknown, but his name too joined the long list at Southsea.

LEADING SEAMAN ERNEST EDGAR NEWNHAM

Newnham was the best friend of Colin Barnard's grandfather, the late Major H. W. G. Cooper and Barnard remembers that 'He always spoke very warmly of Ernie and the loss clearly affected him. On the photograph we have of Ernie Newnham, he has written "To Harry, With the best of luck, Ernie". My granddad wrote alongside that inscription "Ernie Newnham, my school pal. He joined the Navy as a boy as I joined the army as a boy in 1924."'

Ernie Newnham was the son of John and Elizabeth Newnham, and was married to Norma May Newnham of Alresford, Hampshire; whether they had any children is unknown, but when he died, Leading Seaman Newnham was twenty-nine. His name also appears at Southsea.

STOKER 2ND CLASS ERNEST EDWARD PERKINS

Ernie Perkins, the son of Ernie and Emma Perkins, was born in either 1918 or 1919 at 13 Stanley Grove, Tottenham, London. His father died when still a relatively young man, however, so young Ernie was brought up by his mother and stepfather, George. His sister, Patty, died in 1939, but his brother, Jack, survived the war. Ernie went to Lancastrian School, played district football and swam for London Boys. In 1938, he joined the Royal Navy with his friend, Doug White, who would later survive the *Royal Oak* disaster. Perkins' first ship was the aircraft carrier HMS *Eagle*, from which he joined *Royal Oak* shortly before the declaration of war. According to his family, Ernie Perkins ended up in the water alive when the ship sank, but was never seen again – yet another name to be seen at Southsea.

64. Boy 1st Class H. H. Hixon. (Bert Pocock).

63. Marine Charles Frederick Hemsley. (Kathryn Trower via Peter Trower).

65. Boy 1st Class John Francis Humber. (Paul Humber).

BOY BUGLER (ROYAL MARINES) AUBREY JOHN PRIESTLEY

One of the youngest 'men' to die on HMS *Royal Oak* was Boy Bugler Priestley, who was only fifteen and from Slough, Buckinghamshire. Jim Sholl remembers:

My close friend John Priestley and I were both Royal Marine Boy Buglers, aged fifteen, in 1939. We were both fairly smart and one day were sent for by the Bugle Major who said that we had been chosen to be Easter Guards (whilst the rest were on leave) and after which we would go on the Royal Tour to the 1939 World Fair in America (on the escort ship HMS *Glasgow*). John took his best dress uniform home on our leave period for his mother to alter the collar, but unfortunately he lost it on the bus-journey so was unable to make it to the *Glasgow*. Instead, he was on the next draft to HMS *Royal Oak* and subsequently lost his life.

CORPORAL (ROYAL MARINES) HENRY DANIEL JORDAN

From Lockinge in Berkshire, Jordan was twenty-eight when he went down with *Royal Oak*. Jim Sholl remembers him too:

Prior to me leaving on the Royal Tour, a very close family friend, Corporal Daniel Jordan, stopped me in the Drill Shed and begged me to join him on *Royal Oak*, but as I was promised to be interviewed for the Royal Yacht upon completion of the Tour, I declined. Jordan lived permanently with my family and his spare time was devoted to scouting. It was a hard decision for me to make as we were always very close friends. The war breaking out, however, changed many things, so instead of going abroad on the Royal Tour I was drafted to HMS *Victory* instead.

It was there that I greeted the *Royal Oak* survivors and I asked those Royal Marines present regarding the welfare of John Priestley and Daniel Jordan. John was last seen in his hammock, apparently unaware of the situation. Daniel was last seen holding open a red-hot hatch cover, releasing many men. Eventually the heavy hatch cover fell and decapitated him. At the 2002 HMS *Royal Oak* Memorial Service at Southsea, I mentioned this to Father John Eldridge who stopped me by saying that his grandfather was always relating the fact that 'someone' was holding open the hatch cover, and that he was the last to escape before it collapsed. Daniel's actions deserved the Victoria Cross in my book, or at least some other high recognition.

CHIEF PETTY OFFICER FRANK RANN

Frank Rann was born at Newport, on the Isle of Wight, on 26 July 1905, entering Boy Service with the Royal Navy in 1921. On 28 July 1938, Rann was awarded the Long Service & Good Conduct Medal, by which time he also had three Good Conduct Badges. Between the wars, he served on many ships, notably HMS *Hood* and HMS *Revenge*. On 21 January 1939, he was posted to HMS *Royal Oak*, and was promoted to Chief Petty Officer aboard that battleship on 31 May. The husband of Jessie, the Chief Petty Officer wrote to his wife shortly before he lost his life:

> 24 Mess
> HMS *Royal Oak*
> c/o GPO London
> Wed 11th October 1939
>
> My Dear,
>
> Sorry to have broken off in a hurry last Sunday. We've been places since then. Once again if you listen to the radio news, it's not far wrong. You have heard that some of our ships had a few odd arguments with German aircraft 'somewhere in the North Sea'. The BBC said so and they're right in their reports. We didn't all find them or they us so we had a more-or-less fool's errand. It's been a beast of weather. There's been a wind for well over a week now, and can it blow this way. Made things very much from pleasant. That applies to the Hun as well as us of course, and I've an idea that we can stick it a bit better than he can. Not that I'm anything of a sailor, but we have always done more time at sea than they have, and it's sea time that makes sailors. The worst of these spasms is that they come suddenly. It's a case of up and away and always being ready to.

66. Petty Officer Arthur Kersey. (Wally Kersey).

67. Ordinary Seaman Douglas Manwaring and Stoker 1st Class Richard William Manwaring, with their brother Cyril. (Alan and Elaine Holloway).

It's not really cold yet, but when there's a lot of air in a hurry, it makes it feel cold. I was glad to have the sweater and if you ever cussed whilst you were knitting it you can find consolation in the fact that it's just 'the thing' in the current circumstances.

Many thanks for your letter of last Wednesday that I got today. That's a week on the way, but I couldn't get it earlier. It's the one in which you enclosed your Dad's four collars, if you have forgotten by the time you get this. He's a funny old toffer, isn't he? Writes as good as gold and it's a pity that we know him or we could get a much better picture of him from his letter. Still, I am sorry for him, he must feel pretty desolate. For so many years, he'd always depended on Mum that now he must be in a continual dream. He doesn't sound at all enthusiastic about continuing alone for long. Perhaps it would be best in the long run for him to pop off nice and peacefully. Funny old Toff about that from Fran.

I suppose he'd like to help, but doesn't know how. Then again, he's just as likely to have thoughts in his head about what little money Mum had. That's not very charitable on my part and I'd better stop. It's different trying to put things on paper than it would be if I was in that chair opposite you. Wish I was. That chair and you seem a long way away, and if there was the least inkling of when I should be there again, the time would seem to go twice as pleasantly.

This blooming war doesn't improve, does it? True we haven't seen anything of it yet, nor have you, thank goodness. But there's always the thought that you or I may see it anytime. That's just what it's all about, I s'pose. To put an end to the feeling that we might be 'at it' any time. So let's hope that we can put up with the waiting and wondering until it's over and then enjoy the feeling that we can plan ahead a bit. How many times have you said – 'the blooming dictators seem determined to upset our plans'? So they have, first over your trip to Malta and ever since – bad cess to 'em.

It's a week ago last Sat, or a fortnight this, since I trod on terra firma. There's not much to do when I can go, except the walk and maybe a couple of pints. But it's very acceptable when it does come. Makes us chaps laugh when we read in some belated paper that the poor militia somewhere are complaining that they have to walk two miles to camp after the pubs chuck out in the dark. And that all the talent on the West-end stages are falling over one another to amuse the lads. By Gum! I could work up a good old grouse. Still, that was always our privilege and I'm not going to let you in on it. You could do the same I'll be bound, and if we ever get hold of a darn dictator, he's in for a grand time.

It's good news to get another letter saying young Jimmie is still going ahead. S'pect it's the cooler weather coming in again that helps. He's like his father – full-blooded, and with mother feeding him on the fat of the land, he's inclined to get overheated. Says me being the doctor. May be something to do with him going off colour, though you know, Jo. Let him continue the good work then I shan't know my big son when I do see him again. They'll be talking plain soon. You won't notice, but I bet I should see a difference even now. What is it? Three months – or very nearly, and they do change so quickly. Look after 'em, Jo.

Above Left: 68. Stoker Tom Osborne. (Mrs Kate Hooper),

Abobe Right: 69. Able Seaman Charles John Palmer. (Mike Merrison).

70. Leading Seaman Ernest Edgar Newnham. (Colin Barnard).

Above Left: 71. Stoker 2nd Class Ernest Edward Perkins. (H. A. Minors).

Above Right: 73. Chief Petty Officer Frank Rann. (Peter Gisborne).

72. Boy Bugler (Royal Marines) Aubrey John Priestley. (Jim Sholl).

Bad luck having diphtheria in the vicinity. You will get that immunization done, won't you? It must be worth it. Down at the orphanage they were most insistent about it and although those kids went to all the usual schools, there was very little infection. I've wondered how all those kids are getting on. Whether they are evacuated and where. Some of my messmates have their children away from home and those who haven't wish they had. Those women think they are doing best by staying in Pompey and keeping the kids with them but they don't know what worry they cause their old men. Thank goodness you are well set-up and there's nothing to worry over. A chap has just said that his wife says that she's allowed two ton of coal a year. Is that your allowance, or haven't you been told? We use more than that I'm sure. If it is, I can see Mrs. R. doing some wood gathering and very good exercise too. What with knitting socks for the family and writing letters to the old man you'll be getting fat! And don't forget those spring cabbage, because if I happened to get down during the spring I should want something out of the garden and I should appreciate some grown by mother. Anyway, it's everyone's duty to 'grow more grub' says me.

Are you listening to Gracie? I am whilst scribbling this. That wireless is both a god-send and a curse. It gives us news which we don't get from anywhere else, except just around where we are. And amusement 'sometimes'. At other times I get like you do about it. I would advise you to listen to one news a day – up to now the BBC has been first and correct with everything to do with the Navy. They don't scaremonger and if they don't give details it's because they can't for some very good reason. Take these last few days, where we were we heard rumours that some of our ships had been in action but it wasn't until we heard the BBC news that we knew for sure.

Another thing Jo, I'd be very interested in anything around you. I know you don't get about much, but if you happen across any RN news, you'll let me know, won't you? Seems a pity that there's any coldness with Mrs Riley and co. just imagination I should think unless you women-folk are more peculiar than I credit. T'was no false alarm about our Mary, then. Bad luck on the lass that she had to wait until a war came along and her man was away. We're still counting ourselves lucky, aren't we? Goodness knows what will happen when and if this phantom leave comes along. Better make up our minds now for lots and lots of scares. That's what wives are for – to give a bloke lots to talk about, what with large families and small pay-days.

I never commented on your encounter with that sheep-dog at Will's that time. That was just about the tin lid of a 'ell of a week. Don't know that I should altogether seek an encounter with a bloomin' great bobtail after dark on his own ground, so I can fully sympathise with you. S'pect it took a couple of years off your life which means I shall get the insurance so much quicker.

Look, Jo, suppose I packed some washing and sent it along, would you be pleased or otherwise? It's sheets, shirts and collars and the like that want a good boil. Here there's no chance of anything but rubbing it out and drying it in some enclosed artificially heated place, and you know what happens after a few turns of that. Please say if you think the weather is against it or you have plenty to do otherwise.

Now it's post time. That dream of yours about a house and so on will come true one day, old pal. For the present, all my love. Tons of it, or rather gallons.

Ta Ta.

Frank.

By the time Mrs Rann read the foregoing, she was already a widow. On 14 October, Rear Admiral Lait wrote to her, expressing his 'very deep regret' having learned of Frank's death, offering the 'sincerest sympathy of the officers and men of the Royal Navy'.

Left to raise two small children alone, on just seven shillings apiece, when the spirited Mrs Rann received her husband's medals in 1951, she threw them straight in the bin, saying 'I can't feed hungry children on them!'

For the record, Chief Petty Officer Frank Rann is remembered at Southsea and was awarded the 1939-45 Star, the Atlantic Star and the War Medal.

LEADING SEAMAN LESLEY GORDON SQUIRES

Squires was born at Bournemouth, Dorset, on 19 August 1906, the son of Robert and Harriet Squires, joining the Royal Navy at Portsmouth on 15 November 1924. Like Frank Rann, Gordon Squires was a seaman of experience, having also served aboard various ships before joining HMS *Royal Oak* on 7 June 1939; he had also received the Long Service & Good Conduct Medal and three Good Conduct badges. Married to Nellie, his son, Robert, remembers:

When *Royal Oak* was sunk I was just a fifteen-month-old baby living in Eastleigh, Hampshire, with my mother. After father's death and the blitz started we were evacuated to a village in Nottinghamshire. Mother married again when I was twelve years old, so it was around forty years later that my stepfather died and mother talked to me about my real father. The trigger to those discussions was often her visits to the HMS *Royal Oak* Association's October reunions, which we discovered around 1980. At the reunions I met three men who had known my father, although sadly all are now deceased and my mother died twenty years ago.

On leaving school, my father was employed as a bank clerk, but he quickly tired of this and signed on as a fifteen-year-old Boy Sailor. He met my mother at a dance in New Cross, celebrating the 'freedom' given to HMS *Deptford*. Soon afterwards he left on a three-year tour of the Persian Gulf but they married soon after his return. As a Boy or young sailor he represented the Navy in demonstrations and would stand on top of the mast, I think he once did this at Earl's Court.

On the day before the sinking, he was scheduled to be promoted to Acting Petty Officer, apparently this was the way the Navy did such things, confirmation in the rank coming six months later. He was killick on 'B' Deck, cox of the ship's lifeboat and manned a gun, also on 'B' Deck.

Mother heard about the ship's loss from the milkman, who was collecting cash for the week's milk, but had no official confirmation until some days afterwards.

CHIEF PETTY OFFICER COOK WILLIAM SMALL

Keith Small remembers his father's loss:

He was born in Southampton, one of six children, two boys and four girls. My mother was also from Southampton but after they married my parents went to live in Portsmouth, and thence to Fareham, where I spent all my childhood. When *Royal Oak* was lost, my mother was left with three children: my brother, Roy, was eight, I was five and my sister, Shirley, was four.

I can remember that when the bad news came through on the radio, our neighbours on either side came dashing round to our home. I also remember the local policeman coming to the door with news that father had been lost.

As you can imagine, things were hard with three young children to bring up. My mother had to go out to work and also took in lodgers. My mother also lost her parents in the war when their house in Southampton was bombed. Shortly after the war my brother was taken ill with TB, spent the next ten years in and out of hospital, eventually dying in 1956. That hit my mother very hard, it was bad losing her husband, but at that time she knew that she had to pull herself together and raise the family. From Roy's death onwards she had poor health and died of cancer in 1963; my sister also died of it in 1984. I have a cousin, Patricia, daughter of my father's sister, Dolly. We are the only survivors of our small family. We always attend the *Royal Oak* reunions with our spouses.

William Small is remembered at Southsea.

Above Left: 74. Leading Seaman Lesley George Squires. (Robert Squires).

Above Right: 75. Chief Petty Officer Cook William Small. (Keith Small).

76. Boy 1st Class Harry Spencer. (Mr and Mrs A. Gamble).

BOY 1ST CLASS HARRY SPENCER

Harry Spencer was seventeen when he died that terrible night in Scapa Flow. From Mexborough, in Yorkshire, the local newspaper reported his death as follows:

Last Saturday morning, Mrs G. Spencer, of 26 Dryden Road, Mexborough, received a letter from her son, Harry, on board HMS *Royal Oak*. With it was a note from a shipmate, George Stephen; both wrote of the happy Christmas leave they were so much looking forward to in Mexborough, and Stephen of his warm appreciation of Mrs Spencer's invitation. Later in the day Mrs Spencer heard the first announcement of the sinking of the battleship, and early on Monday morning, learned from the War Office that her son had lost his life. Stephen was among the survivors.

This is the tragic story of what is probably Mexborough's first war casualty. Spencer, who was the eldest son of Mr & Mrs George Spencer, was seventeen and a half; he had been in the Navy since he was sixteen. When the *Royal Oak* was re-commissioned earlier this year, he volunteered for service aboard her and his acceptance realised for him one of his greatest ambitions.

During his comparatively short naval career, Spencer had often written home of his happiness in his new sphere. A former pupil at Adwick Road School, he worked at Mexborough brickyard and Denaby Main Colliery before joining up on the day following his sixteenth birthday. He went aboard the training ship *Caledonia* at Rosyth, and worked his way to the rank of Petty Officer Boy. He joined the *Royal Oak* in March of this year, and had attained the rank of First Class Boy. There are five brothers and two sisters. His father went through the Great War without a scratch, serving with the artillery.

Spencer's last letter home told his mother that he was very well and happy. She told me that he and Stephen were such good pals that she can only assume that the latter must have been on duty and her son asleep when the explosions occurred. The appearance of Stephen's name among the survivors increased her anxiety until the War Office

Charges to pay
_____ s. _____ d.
RECEIVED .

No. 0047

OFFICE STAMP

26. JX 158255 ++ OFFICE

TELEGRAM

Prefix. Time handed In. Office of Origin and Service Instructions. Words.

84

84   1.5 PORTSMOUTH T OHMS 29

To _____

MRS EMMA SPENCER 26 BRYDEN RD MEXBOROUGH YORKS =

DEEPLY REGRET TO REPORT DEATH OF YOUR SON HARRY SPENCER
BOY JX 158255 ON WAR SERVICE =

= REAR ADMIRAL R N BARRACKS PORTSMOUTH +

For free repetition or doubtful words telephone " TELEGRAMS ENQUIRY " or call, with this form
at office of delivery. Other enquiries should be accompanied by this form and, if possible, the envelope.

77. The telegram reporting Harry Spencer's death.

78. Assistant Cook Mark Warren
Stephens. (Via Sara Frith).

79. Stoker 2nd Class Leonard George
Trussler. (Kay Howarth).

80. Able Seaman Joseph Pascal Wilkins. (Mr Bryan Wilkins).

81. Wilkins aboard the *Royal Oak*. (Mr Bryan Wilkins).

communication arrived with its unhappy news. She is very grateful for the many kind messages of sympathy received. A memorial service is to be held in the parish church on Sunday evening.

A trained gunner, Harry Spencer had last been home on leave the previous Whitsun, but never got to enjoy the Christmas of 1939, which he was so looking forward to. His name is recorded on the Southsea Memorial.

ASSISTANT COOK MARK WARREN STEPHENS

Stephens was the son of Mark and Martha Stephens, and the husband of Daisy Ellen Stephens, of Wareham, Dorset. Sara Frith wrote to me about the great-uncle she never met:

When visiting my Nan a couple of weeks ago I had a brilliant discussion about our family history and, of course, Mark, whose photograph has been in Nan's lounge for as long as I can remember. Mark was her only brother and they were very close. Upon return from Southampton I did some further research and found that Mark is commemorated on the Portsmouth Naval Memorial, a fact of which, even after all this time, my Nan was unaware. So last weekend my sister and I took Nan, who is in a wheelchair and ninety next March, to a very tearful reunion at the Memorial. Many tears were shed but my Nan feels at last someone is interested. I took my laptop down and showed her your website and she asked me to email you Mark's picture and details.

Mark was born in Southampton on 22 September 1917, a month after his father was killed aboard the ammunition ship SS *Wisbech*, serving in the Mercantile Marine during the Great War. Mark had two sisters, my Nan, Lydia, and Kate.

Mark originally worked on the Royal Mail Line's ship *Alcantara*, but was transferred to the Royal Navy when war broke out. He served as Assistant Chef on *Royal Oak* and was twenty-two when he died. Mark had actually got married a few weeks before, but his wife later re-married.

My Nan has now asked that when the time comes her ashes are scattered at Scapa Flow, although she doesn't want to go anywhere near the water, as she doesn't like it, although her father, brother and husband have all been given to the sea.

STOKER 2ND CLASS LEONARD GEORGE TRUSSLER

The son of George and Rhoda Trussler, of Liphook in Hampshire, very little is known of this casualty, although his sister, Kay Howarth, remembers that:

Sadly he was only nineteen when he died, so he had a lot of life ahead of him to live.

I remember him as a very happy person, always teasing me as brother and sister do. He liked to caddie at our local golf course. I was only twelve when he died, and am now seventy-nine, so my memory is not as bright as once it was.

Trussler is also commemorated on the Portsmouth Naval Memorial.

ABLE SEAMAN JOSEPH PASCAL WILKINS

Wilkins was another seaman of some considerable experience lost aboard HMS *Royal Oak*. Born in Wantage, Berkshire, on 7 April 1904, the son of James and Emily Wilkins, before entering the Royal Navy for Boy Service on 23 July 1921, he had served in the Mercantile Marine. He received his Long Service & Good Conduct Medal on 2 July 1937.

His son, Bryan Wilkins, expands upon these basic details:

My father was the youngest son, born in a small house in Wallingford Street, Wantage. His father was a Master Confectioner. At the age of seventeen, he joined the Royal Navy and went to HMS *Vivid* (Devonport Barracks).

In 1926 he was posted to HMS *Victory* at Portsmouth, where he met my mother, Ada Margaret Oughton. They married on 13 April 1927, and later that year my sister, Betty, was born. My eldest brother, George, was born on 20 May 1932, again while father was serving on HMS *Victory*. I was born on 17 September 1938, whilst he was at Whale Island Gunnery School.

On 1 June 1939, father joined HMS *Royal Oak*. I was just thirteen months old when he lost his life for King and country, aboard *Royal Oak*, at Scapa Flow.

After my father's death we were bombed out of our home in Brompton Road: a mine was dropped opposite and demolished a house, ours was blasted to bits. At the time we were in shelters hidden under Portsdown Hill. Most of our possessions and furniture were lost, because of the heavy bombing. My brother, sister and I were evacuated to Winchester where we stayed with the Kitt family for some months.

Because of difficult times my mother had little or no possessions and little or no money, with the exception of her small widow's pension, so she married my stepfather, Percy Reid, in 1941. Apparently Percy, who was employed as a skilled labourer in the Dockyard, had known my father during his posting to Portsmouth.

With the exception of my father, our family survived the bombing and war years.

Able Seaman Wilkins was thirty-six when he died, and is remembered at Southsea.

STOKER FIRST CLASS LEONARD GEORGE WREN

Wren was a thirty-nine-year-old married man from Portland, Dorset, with two sons. Another experienced seaman, between the wars he served on HMS *Revenge*, HMS *Iron Duke* and HMS *Enchantress*.

Unique amongst the casualties recorded in this book, he lies buried in the Lyness Royal Naval Cemetery at Scapa Flow. The bodies of just thirty-four *Royal Oak* casualties were recovered from the sea, all of which were buried at Lyness, and eight of which are unidentified.

Of course many of those who were fortunate to survive the sinking of HMS *Royal Oak* would lose their lives on active service before the war was over. An example of such a casualty is Royal Marine Sergeant John Joseph Coombes, known by his family as 'Ian'; his widow, Dorothy, shares with us her memories of what happened:

Ian joined *Royal Oak* in 1939 – a few months before the outbreak of war. At that time we were married with a daughter and son. Ian felt that war was imminent. He was anxious that we should not remain in Portsmouth which city would be in danger zone for war if it should arise, so he accepted his Aunt's offer to have us at her home near Petersfield while he was at sea. We came to Sheet (*a village near Petersfield*) a few days before war was declared.

On Saturday, 14 October 1939, Auntie May went shopping in the town, nearly two miles away, and while there heard the news that one of our ships had been sunk and the name of the ship. As we were in a country area she had to walk to town as we had no transport. She arrived breathless and exhausted because she didn't want me to be alone with the children when the news came on the radio at lunchtime.

Upon seeing her in such a state after her long walk – I suspected bad news, and when I said 'Not the *Royal Oak*?', she nodded in the affirmative.

So early in the war the shock was terrible and I hoped it wasn't true. But it was on the radio, so there was no doubt.

I can remember how stunned I was and picked up my nine-month-old son, and just wandered round the garden for hours. Later that evening two visitors arrived – they were from a greengrocer shop in Petersfield. My mother-in-law as Ian's next of kin had been informed that Ian was safe, so they had received the news from her and came to Sheet to let me know. They had a telephone which was a rare luxury in those days.

The shock brought me to floods of tears of joy, but next morning in the Sunday newspaper the name Coombes was there, but the initials wrong – so again I was in doubt until later I received a telegram just to say 'All's well', so I knew he had survived, and looked forward to his coming home.

At the time of sinking Ian was twenty-six years of age. I was twenty-five years old and the children (daughter) two years and (son) nine months.

Eventually he arrived home to Sheet – but was a changed man for a while, and wouldn't talk about it to the family. He had received a shock. At the time of the ship being hit while in harbour he was on night watch and when the order came to abandon ship he jumped into the sea, and being a good swimmer was able to assist a sailor who was a non-swimmer. They used a piece of debris for support and then when he realised the sailor had died he continued to swim. That was another shock. Eventually he reached shore. I never knew how. It so happened that his duty period had saved his life for the *Royal* Marines' Mess Deck had received a direct hit.

82. Stoker First Class George Wren, pictured with his wife at home in Portland during his final leave. (Mrs J. Mason).

Below Left: 83. The grave of an unidentified member of *Royal Oak's* ship's company at Lyness.

Below Right: 84. Wren's grave at Lyness Naval Cemetery.

85. Sergeant (Royal Marines) John Joseph 'Ian' Coombes with his wife, Dorothy. (Mike Coombes).

In due course Ian worked in Portsmouth Eastney Barracks – then had a period as training instructor of 'small arms' and then Derby where he trained men on Anti-Aircraft fire. Then at the end of 1940, he had news that he would be going to sea again – destination unknown – and the last time we ever saw him was the end of December 1940. He had arranged with me a code by which I would know where he was (in aerogrammes) so I knew that he was in Crete, and it was in the evacuation of Crete that he was posted 'missing'.

At that time I kept my children's memories of their father alive. Obviously I didn't tell anyone about his destination for security reasons. Sadly it wasn't until after the war 1945 that I was able to let anyone know – so Ian's parents (senior Salvation Army Officers running naval and military homes) advertised for information in the *Globe and Laurel (the Royal Marines' magazine)*.

86. The graves at Lyness of those lost with *Royal Oak* and fortunate enough to have a known resting place, although not all are identified.

Ian had survived the period of German aircraft bombing, and was being evacuated to Alexandria on a ship which had a direct hit – HMS *Hereward* – in May 1941, and Ian was last seen on that ship.

How I wish that Ian could have seen our wonderful family now. Our children are now grandparents. All have university degrees and Michael (my son) after naval service etc. was made an OBE for Naval Duties in a civilian capacity after retirement.

Sadly, Sergeant Coombes name joined those of his shipmates lost with HMS *Royal Oak* on the Memorial at Southsea.

To conclude this chapter, the reader should reflect upon this poignant fact: there are thirty-one former members of HMS *Royal Oak*'s ship's company remembered here, all ordinary sailors or non-commissioned officers; a further 802 officers and men lost their lives on HMS *Royal Oak*; the bodies of 799 were never found.

6
No Flowers on a Sailor's Grave

On 10 May 1940, Hitler unleashed *blitzkrieg* against the West, astonishingly defeating Holland, Belgium, Luxembourg and France in just six weeks. By the beginning of June, the British Expeditionary Force had been evacuated from Dunkirk, and the Nazi empire stretched from the Baltic to the English Channel. This provided the U-boats with bases along France's western coast, such as at St Nazaire, La Pallice and Lorient, conveniently situated to strike at enemy shipping in the Bay of Biscay. In August 1940, Karl Dönitz became leader of the new U-Boat Command, his headquarters at Lorient. Now was the time for his theories on submarine warfare to become reality.

U-boats located convoys and then, using excellent radio communications, informed Lorient. U-Boat Command then signalled other patrolling boats, directing them into the area of operations. Consequently, many boats were concentrated together, so that when a convoy was attacked by these so-called 'Wolf Packs', maximum destruction was achieved. Contrary to popular belief, U-boats actually attacked on the surface, by night, and the autumn of 1940 became known as the 'Happy Time': U-boats were sinking an average of five-and-a-half ships per month.

Slowly, the British perfected submarine detection and destruction tactics and weapons, and the 'Happy Time' came to an abrupt end in the spring of 1941.

In the March of that fateful year, three of the top U-boat 'aces' were sunk in the North Atlantic: U-47 failed to return from a North Atlantic patrol and was presumed lost with all hands. The great Otto Kretschmer's famous boat, the U-99, known as the 'Golden Horseshoe', was destroyed on 17 March, 'Silent Otto' being captured. On the same day, Joachim Schepke and his U-100 were lost.

On that last fateful patrol, Prien had once more found a convoy and notched up another 22,000 tons. A flurry of signals to Lorient described the action, but when his position was requested on 8 March, Prien failed to respond. Anxious hours passed into days as Dönitz and his staff waited and prayed for news, hoping that Prien's silence was simply due to a broken radio. After a few days, U-47 was still missing, and Lorient received a signal from the *Führerhauptquartier* that news of Prien's likely loss was to be kept top secret, indeed, not even the crew's next of kin were to be notified. Six weeks after U-47 had slipped her moorings and headed for the North Atlantic, Frau Prien, concerned that her husband had not yet returned, called Admiral von Friedeburg for news. The Admiral, knowing of Hitler's order, could tell her nothing, so the concerned lady simply assumed that her husband had again been sent on some kind of secret mission.

By the middle of April, however, U-47 was still both silent and missing. Still Hitler refused permission for the news to be released and next of kin informed, such a blow to German pride and morale was Prien's loss considered. It was not until the end of that month relatives were informed, but even then only on the express understanding that the news was absolutely top secret. It was common knowledge amongst dockyard workers and the like, however, that U-47 had not returned, so inevitably the news leaked out. Only on 23 May 1941, ten weeks after U-47 was lost, was a radio announcement was made admitting the loss of Prien and his crew.

The suppression of this bad news, however, gave rise to wild rumours in Germany: the most persistent, emanating from the Military Academy, was that Prien and his crew had mutinied against the Nazi regime and been sent to the dreaded Russian front to fight with a penal battalion!

88. *Korvettenkapitän* Otto Kretschmer, captured when his U-99 was destroyed by the Royal Navy, like U-47, in March 1941.

87. Dönitz was promoted to Rear Admiral and made Commander-in-Chief of the *Ubootwaffe* after U-47's victorious mission to Scapa Flow. It was his tactics and strategies that led to the U-boats being so successful in the Battle of the Atlantic. After Hitler committed suicide in 1945, Dönitz actually became his successor, and was *Führer* for a few days whilst Germany's surrender was arranged with the Allies. When he died in 1981, his funeral was attended by thousands of old comrades, including 100 holders of the Knight's Cross, such was the affection and high esteem in which the 'Old Lion' was held.

89. *Kaleun* Joachim Schepke, another top U-boat 'Tonnage King', also lost in March 1941, which signalled the end of the so-called 'Happy Time'.

So widely did this rumour circulate that the High Command had to issue a formal statement of denial. After the war, when rumours of all kinds concerning goings on during the war years were rife, a letter appeared in the *Braunschweiger Zeitung* newspaper by a former German soldier, Hellmut Kuckat, recently released from captivity in Siberia, who claimed that Prien had been killed fighting on the Wolchow. A friend of Prien's, he claimed, showed him a snapshot of the great submariner's grave, who, this correspondent claimed, had been sent to a penal battalion with his entire crew for making false claims of sinkings and accumulated tonnage. Surviving friends of Prien, anxious to dispel this latest story, contacted Kuckat and concluded that he was telling this story in good faith. Other rumours regarding Prien's fate included that he had been court-martialled for refusing to put to sea in an unseaworthy boat, sent to the military prison in Torgau before ending up starved or executed at the Esterwegen concentration camp. Prien's friends, including Wolfgang Frank, a former officer on Dönitz's staff who had twice sailed with Prien, decided that the only way to deal with these rumours was to contact the British Admiralty and ascertain exactly what had really become of the 'Bull of Scapa Flow'.

The official history of the Battle of the Atlantic, prepared for the Admiralty and Air Ministry by the Central Office of Information in 1946, confirmed beyond reasonable doubt that U-47 had been sunk on 7 March 1941, by the corvettes *Camellia* and *Arbutus*, and the destroyer *Wolverine*. Frank, together with the former Nazi propagandist who had written up Prien's wartime memoir, published a booklet in 1949, called 'What Really Happened to Prien?'. In 1954, Frank published an expanded version of the book, a biography of Prien, as a paperback, which was translated and also distributed in England. So it was that the true fate of U-47 became known and accepted throughout the world. In more recent times, however, further research has suggested that HMS *Wolverine* did not, in fact, attack U-47 but Hans Eckermann's U-A (one of the boats built for Turkey before the war) which survived the incident.

90. At Laboe in Germany, a Type VIIC U-boat, the U-995, is preserved as a memorial to the *Ubootwaffe*. As Allied air power increasingly threatened the U-boats as war progressed, anti-aircraft defences were improved by the addition of another platform to the bridge's *Wintergarten* to accommodate a further 20 mm cannon. Ostensibly, this is the only obvious external difference between this boat and the Type VIIB U-47, so U-995 provides an excellent opportunity to experience the kind of vessel in which Prien penetrated Scapa Flow and sank HMS *Royal Oak*.

We can never, therefore, be certain of Prien's exact fate, which was either attributable to the two corvettes *Camillia* and *Arbutus,* or possibly to an internal explosion of her own mines. U-47's last known position was 60.00N/19.0W, near the Rockall Banks.

Whatever really was the cause of their demise, for Prien and his crew, like those who died aboard HMS *Royal Oak,* their fate was to be consumed by the sea, the cold, black depths their grave and no marker to commemorate them having passed through this life. It has often been said that there are no victors in war, and the loss of U-47 seems to forcibly reinforce that fact. Indeed, these poignant lines appear an appropriate epitaph to all of those lost at sea and who have no known grave:

No flowers on a sailor's grave
No lilies on an ocean wave
Their only tribute the seagulls sweep
And the tear drop on a loved one's cheek

Postscript

The Scapa Flow anchorage, where the North Sea and Atlantic meet, was effectively the Royal Navy's equivalent of America's Pearl Harbor in the Pacific. There, on 7 December 1941, the Japanese also made a surprise attack, this time by air and before war between the two countries was even declared, achieving absolutely devastating results of an unprecedented magnitude. One lone U-boat could never have achieved such destruction, but had the Home Fleet not been dispersed literally in the nick of time, U-47 would undoubtedly have destroyed much more than one ageing battleship. Today, the ghosts of Pearl Harbor remain beneath the sea, visible in the gin-clear tropical water, moving memorials to the hundreds of men who went down on their ships. So too is the case with HMS *Royal Oak*, the wreck of which remains in Scapa Bay, just 1,000 yards offshore.

Between the wars, the German High Seas Fleet, scuttled at Scapa Flow in 1919, was heavily salved in a massive operation lasting a number of years. The construction of such ships includes various valuable metals, such as bronze and brass, hence the salvers' interest. As these ships were not lost in action, and as they are not therefore the underwater tombs of yesterday's warriors, there is nothing morally wrong with this. The same could not be said, however, of UB-116, the watery grave of *Leutnant* Emsmann and his crew. In 1919, Emsmann's boat, containing the dead crew, was raised, but foundered in Hoxa Sound, off the island of Flotta.

91. The Royal Naval Memorial at Portsmouth (Southsea), scene of a moving service every October at which the HMS *Royal Oak* Association remembers lost shipmates.

92. The service is taken by the Revd Ron Patterson, MBE, who served aboard HMS *Hood* between the wars.

In 1969, the wreck was sold by the Ministry of Defence to a private salvage company, and the rotting hulk broken up into smaller sections by explosives. This can only be considered an officially sanctioned defilement of what was clearly a war grave: had UB-116 been a navigation hazard then interference with it may have been justified, but salvage, the only motive, cannot be considered morally acceptable. The discovery of large quantities of oil beneath the North Sea, however, led to Flotta becoming an oil terminal, meaning that oil had to be piped there from North Sea rigs. With this in mind, it became necessary to detonate the live torpedoes known to remain on the seabed with UB-116, which was done without delay. In 2005, I dived UB-116, in good visibility, and, not surprisingly, found the wreck extremely broken up, a mass of twisted pipes, wires and plates, although the hydroplanes could be identified and, a little way from the main wreckage, what appeared to be the conning tower's remains. When I dived the wreck, it was with the interest of a professional historian, to lay eyes on the last U-boat lost in the Great War, which was a great experience, one that was undertaken with great respect by all of our diving team. Nothing was taken from the wreck, and, quite rightly, all of Scapa's wrecks are now protected by statute as ancient monuments (the same legislation protecting Stonehenge, in fact).

In 1951, the Ministry of Defence undertook a survey of HMS *Royal Oak*, recovering in the process the ship's valuable propellers. In December 1957 – the same year that Scapa Flow closed as a Royal Navy anchorage – the Ministry invited tenders for the scrapping and salvage of the wreck, which, given the huge quantity of human remains undoubtedly still present within the wreck at that time, cannot have any moral justification whatsoever. Indeed, and quite rightly, a storm of public protest followed, accusing the authorities of deliberate desecration. The Admiralty therefore had no choice but to abandon the enterprise.

After the war, from the 1960s onwards, scuba diving became accessible to the masses and, as equipment and techniques improved, recreational diving became increasingly popular. Not surprisingly, the impressive wrecks remaining at Scapa Flow became regularly visited by divers from all over Europe, if not the world. Unfortunately, in those days, there was very much a souvenir-gathering culture amongst divers, and brass objects like portholes became extremely desirable objects. Consequently, a great deal of (inexcusable) damage was done to wrecks all over the British Isles by lump-hammer-wielding 'wreckers'.

93. Ron Patterson when a Boy sailor aboard HMS *Hood*.

94. Mrs Kate Hooper points to her brother's name on the Southsea Memorial, Stoker Tom Osborne, lost with HMS *Royal Oak*, aged nineteen.

Unfortunately, this was also the case with HMS *Royal Oak*. With no law to restrict or prohibit diving on such wrecks, regardless of the circumstances in which they sank, divers frequently visited the site, and local diving schools even used the wreck for training purposes, given its relatively shallow location. At this time, one particular diver even removed the great brass letters spelling 'Royal Oak' from the ship's bow, but years later, after the opening of the former Lyness pumping station as a museum, this individual had a pang of conscience and donated those precious items, which are now displayed there.

95. Survivor Kenneth Toop, the indefatigable secretary of the HMS *Royal Oak* Association, at the 2004 service.

If it was unacceptable for the Ministry of Defence to interfere with such wrecks, it was equally, if not more so, for civilian recreational divers to do so. Not surprisingly, the relatives of casualties were opposed to such disturbance, and quite rightly so.

In 1986, all this changed when the Protection of Military Remains Act was introduced.

96. Mr Paul Humber proudly pointing out his brother's name, Boy 1st Class John Francis Humber.

97. Survivor Bert Pocock at Southsea, 2004.

98. Tributes to lost souls.

This statute designated certain sites as 'protected places', including the crash sites of aircraft whose aircrews remain 'missing' and wrecks such as the *Royal Oak*. Thanks to this legislation, such sites, where human remains are undoubtedly present, have a new status as official war graves. From that point on, therefore, no unofficial diving or interference was permitted on the *Royal Oak*, and long may that remain the case. Today, above the wreck bobs a green conical buoy proclaiming:

99. Survivors Bert Pocock and Arthur Smith relate their experiences to the author at the 2004 HMS *Royal Oak* Association reunion.

100. A superb artist's impression of the wreck of HMS *Royal Oak* today. (Peter Rowlands, Ocean Optics).

101. A Royal Navy diver hoists the white ensign over the wreck of HMS *Royal Oak*, now covered in soft corals known, appropriately, as 'dead man's fingers'. (Peter Rowlands, Ocean Optics).

102. Responsible wreck diving: the author safely back aboard MV *Halton* after a dive at Scapa Flow. (Lesley Harper).

'This marks the wreck of HMS *Royal Oak* and the grave of her crew. Respect their resting place. Unauthorised diving prohibited.'

Every year, a moving act of remembrance takes place afloat at the *Royal Oak* buoy, attended by survivors, fewer in number as time marches on, and bereaved families. Annually, Royal Navy divers also visit the site, hoisting a white ensign underwater on the wreck, and

103. Irresponsible wreck diving: these brass letters spelling the ship's name were stolen from the wreck by a 'wrecker' who redeemed himself by donating them to the Scapa Flow Visitor Centre at Lyness.

survey what has in recent years become a major environmental issue due to continued seepage of fuel oil.

During the course of my research for this book, I requested permission to accompany the navy divers to the wreck, to gain a first-hand impression of this mighty ship and scale of tragedy. I am a professional historian and a responsible diver. I had a legitimate reason to visit the wreck, with written support from both survivors and the relatives of casualties. The Royal Navy agreed, but then came the extremely disappointing news that the Ministry of Defence had stepped in and vetoed the expedition. Not all divers are souvenir-gathering nuisances, and it is a great shame that the reputation of wreck diving has, in some quarters, deteriorated to this extent, and that divers such as Elwyn Harper and myself are thus negatively affected through absolutely no fault of our own.

Others argue that such wrecks should not be dived as a mark of respect to those who died in that place, but that argument seems weak indeed to me: we can, of course, walk across the sites of land battles where many thousands of men died, indeed, 'battlefield tourism', including commercial guided tours, is now a thriving industry – so what is the difference? Be all that as it may, HMS *Royal Oak* at least lies, for the most part, completely undisturbed in the green and cold waters of Scapa Flow, the somewhat hypocritical Ministry of Defence's mercenary efforts to sell off the wreck for salvage thwarted, and recreational diving prohibited.

Nearly seventy years later, the sinking of HMS *Royal Oak* remains keenly felt amongst Orcadians, some of whom still recall that fateful night. Oil from the ship's vast fuel reserves continues to seep out into the sea, washing up on the shoreline and damaging wildlife. Various initiatives are underway to negate this, but at least that leaking oil also helps remind us *Royal Oak*'s sad loss, and the deaths of 833 men, all with hearts of oak.

Acknowledgements

Firstly, I must thank Mr Kenneth Toop, a survivor of the tragedy and Honorary Secretary of the HMS *Royal Oak* Association, who put me in touch with most of the families from whom contributions to this book were obtained. Without his help this work would have been impossible.

Fellow maritime historian Peter Rowlands initially connected me with the HMS *Royal Oak* Association and promoted my quest for information on his excellent website devoted to the ship.

Naturally, I am equally indebted to all of the relatives of casualties who have provided material, and the survivors for sharing with me their memories of that traumatic night back in 1939.

I would also like to thank the Commonwealth War Graves Commission, Orkney Library, Helmet Maros (a veteran U-boat man), my old diving instructors and friends Elwyn and Lesley Harper and Bob Anderson (skipper of MV *Halton*, Stromness), Chris Gale and James Sarkar.

Bibliography

PRIMARY SOURCES

Author's personal correspondence and interviews with veterans and the relatives of casualties.

SECONDARY SOURCES

Bekker, C., *Hitler's Naval War* (Corgi, London, 1976).

Brown, M., & Meehan, P., *Scapa Flow: The Story of Britain's Greatest Naval Anchorage in the Two World Wars* (The Penguin Press, London, 1968).

Frank, W., *Enemy Submarine* (William Kimber & Co Ltd, London, 1954).

Mallman-Showell, J., *German Navy Handbook 1939-45* (Sutton Publishing, Stroud, 1999).

McKee, A., *Black Saturday*, first edition (Souvenir Press, London, 1966).

Miller, J., *Scapa* (Birlinn Ltd, London, 2000).

Prien, G., *U-boat Commander* (Tempus Publishing, Stroud, 2000).

Rössler, E., *The U-Boat: The Evolution & Technical History of German Submarines* (Arms & Armour Press, London, 1981).

Sharpe, P., *U-boat Fact File: Detailed Service Histories of the Submarines Operated by the Kriegsmarine, 1939-45* (Midland Publishing, Hinckley, 1998).

Smith, P. L., *The Naval Wrecks of Scapa Flow* (The Orkney Press, Kirkwall, 1989).

Stern, R. C., *Type VII U-boats* (Arms & Armour Press, London, 1981).

Weaver, H. J., *Nightmare at Scapa Flow: The Truth About the Sinking of HMS Royal Oak* (Cressrelles Publishing Co. Ltd, Malvern, 1980).

Williams, A., *The Battle of the Atlantic* (BBC Worldwide Ltd, London, 2002).

Williamson, W., *Knights of the Iron Cross, 1939-45* (Blandford Press, London, 1987).

Wood, L., *The Bull & the Barriers: The Wrecks of Scapa Flow* (Tempus Publishing, Stroud, 2000).

INTERNET RESOURCES

www.hmsroyaloak.co.uk – Peter Rowlands' excellent site about the ship.
www.U47.org – Rick Joshua's site dedicated to U-47.
www.u-boat.net – The oracle of all U-boat sites.
www.cwgc.org – The Commonwealth War Grave Commissions' site featuring an essential casualty search facility.

DVD

For an impression of life aboard a U-boat on an operational patrol, see Wolfgang Petersen's *Das Boot*, based upon the factual novel of that name by war correspondent Lothar-Günther Buchheim.

The documentary made by Peter Rowlands about HMS *Royal Oak*, which includes underwater footage of the wreck, is excellent and available from Submerged Publications, 5 Western College Road, Mannarmead, Plymouth, PL4 7AG.

PC GAME

To command your own U-boat during the Battle of the Atlantic, see *Silent Hunter II: WW2 Combat Simulator* (Ubi Soft Entertainment, 2001).

Index

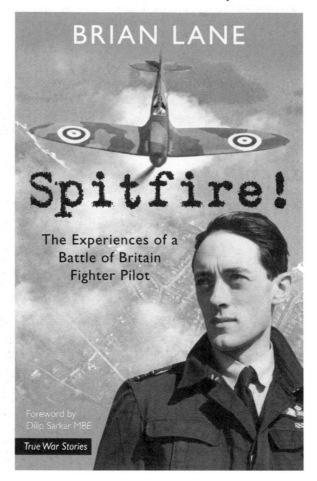

Also available from Amberley Publishing

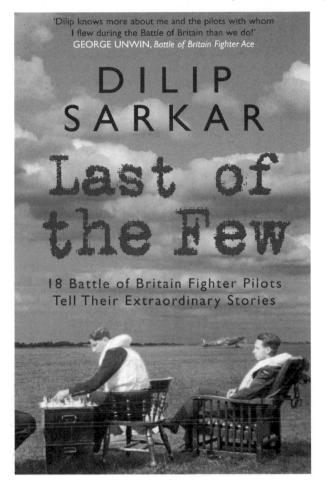

'Dilip knows more about me and the pilots with whom I flew during the Battle of Britain than we do!' GEORGE UNWIN, *Battle of Britain Fighter Ace*

DILIP SARKAR

Last of the Few

18 Battle of Britain Fighter Pilots Tell Their Extraordinary Stories

18 Spitfire and Hurricane fighter pilots recount their experiences of combat during the Battle of Britain

'Dilip knows more about me and the pilots with whom I flew during the Battle of Britain than we do! If anyone ever needs to know anything about the RAF during the summer of 1940, don't ask the Few, ask him!' GEORGE 'GRUMPY' UNWIN, Battle of Britain fighter ace

£20 Hardback
60 illustrations
240 pages
978-1-84868-435-5

Available from all good bookshops or to order direct
Please call **01285-760-030**
www.amberley-books.com

Available from February 2010 from Amberley Publishing

How to fly the legendary fighter plane in combat using the manuals and instructions supplied by the RAF during the Second World War

An amazing array of leaflets, books and manuals were issued by the War Office during the Second World War to aid pilots in flying the Supermarine Spitfire, here for the first time they are collated into a single book with the original 1940s setting. An introduction is supplied by expert aviation historian Dilip Sarkar. Other sections include aircraft recognition, how to act as an RAF officer, bailing out etc.

£9.99 Paperback
40 illustrations
264 pages
978-1-84868-436-2

Available from all good bookshops or to order direct
Please call **01285-760-030**
www.amberleybooks.com

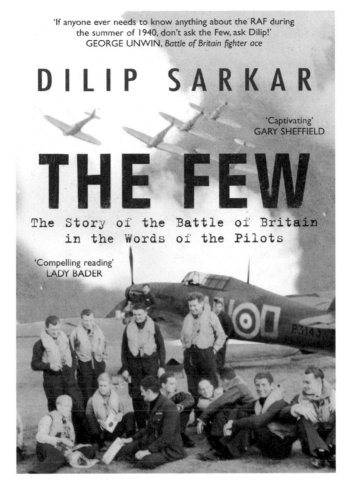

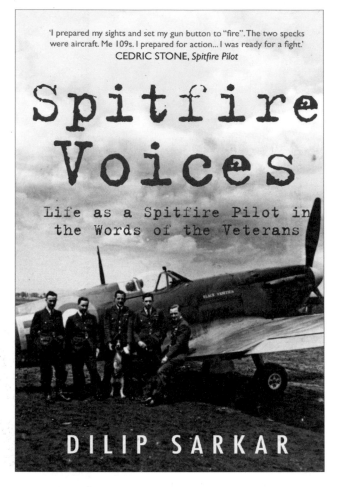